CW00552701

HUNGARY 1956
TWO WORLDS APART

Leo Solti
With George Solti, Nick Solti, and Hugh Thomas

Hungary 1956, Two Worlds Apart

Published by Elite Publishing Academy, Allia Business Centre, Kings Hedges Road, Cambridge, CB4 2HY, United Kingdom
www.ElitePublishingAcademy.com

Cover Design: www.ElitePublishingAcademy.com

First printed 2022. Printed in the United Kingdom, www.ElitePublishingAcademy.com

ISBN Paperback - 978-1-912713-50-9
ISBN eBook - 978-1-912713-49-3

TABLE OF CONTENTS

Introduction 5

Preface - "An Excellent Suggestion" 13

Chapter 1 - Early Years: Acs 15

Chapter 2 - Apprentice Arsonists 29

Chapter 3 - Early Days 35

Chapter 4 – Living Under The Communist Regime 43

Chapter 5 - Budapest 69

Chapter 6 - Joining The Wage-Slaves 103

Goulash Soup a l'Solti 123

Chapter 7 - The Hungarian Revolution, 1956, (More Detail) 141

Chapter 8 – I'm in Heaven 167

Chapter 9 – Reflections: Half-way House 179

Chapter 10 – Aldershot and Fleet 187

Chapter 11 – Making My Way In The New World 199

Chapter 12 – White Lodge 227

Chapter 13 - It's Been A Wonderful Life (26/11/2020) 235

Conclusion 243

Hungary 1956, Two Worlds Apart

Introduction

My Dad had an extraordinary life. Born in Hungary in 1933, his early childhood was idyllic in many ways, Hungary being an independent nation at that point. He then experienced the Nazi occupation during WW2 which was immediately followed by another even more brutal regime under the Russians. In 1956 he became involved in the Hungarian uprising as a freedom fighter against the might of Russia and became an unintentional hero when he assisted many people to escape Hungary, probably saving many lives in the process, before reaching the safety of England as an almost fatally wounded refugee. The intention of this introduction is to outline how this book came about.

My Dad was a very quiet, unassuming man. He was very polite with impeccable manners and was incredibly honest, sometimes too honest for his own good, and certainly for business, but this was a very endearing quality. He was a man who loved family, hard work, gardening, DIY, fencing, tea drinking, a really good laugh and sometimes the odd cider. He was someone who was fiercely thrifty, so left a very insignificant carbon footprint and the word 'technophobe' could easily have been created for him in later life. Maybe 'traditionalist' would be a kinder phrase.

Much to the chagrin of our Hungarian relations when we finally met (myself in 1999), Dad had not taught my sister Bebba, my two brothers Joe and George and I to speak Hungarian when we were growing up. This was a great shame as young children have the ability to learn languages at a younger age and Hungarian is a particularly difficult language to start to learn in later life, particularly when you have already had French, German and even Latin taught at school. Between my siblings and I we only have a limited collection of Hungarian words and phrases to get us by when visiting Hungary, but it seems impossible to string them together into conversational sentences. To me, at least, it always appeared that Dad's past was something mystical and other worldly. He would rarely ever speak of his past, particularly his life in Hungary and the subject seemed almost taboo. The lack of any Hungarian language we had seemed to further fog our connection with Dad's past and the intriguing mystery it seemed to hold.

When any questions were asked about Dad's past and, more importantly, how he came to leave Hungary the answer was always 'the 1956 uprising' and the subject was quickly changed. I liked to try and impress my friends at school and at home by telling them stories about how my Dad came to have bullet wound scars on his upper arm but, not really knowing the exact story, I would make things up, trying to qualify it somehow by using the standard phrase of the 1956 uprising in Hungary. In any case, most of my friends seemed to be very impressed and it gained me some kind of schoolboy kudos.

As my siblings and I became older we began to feel that we needed to know Dad's story. I have known so many people and relations that have led fascinating lives, heavily embroiled in the upheaval of twentieth century history and living through massive change but their stories were never written down or recorded in any way, so their stories are lost forever only to be vaguely recollected by word of mouth by relatives and subsequently altered and eventually lost over generations. Subsequent genealogical research can reveal where people lived, what their employment was, who they married, their children, what wars they fought in etc but the first hand account is still lost. The detail and human connection is missing as its all just official records. Apart from the genuine interest we had for our Dad's story we increasingly didn't want that to happen to our family history. Of course, this fear starts to increase the older people become.

About ten years ago, or so, after a great deal of persistent persuasion (Dad called it nagging) Dad was persuaded to bullet point the events that led to him leaving Hungary. If I remember correctly, it was George that managed to achieve this and I believe that a certain amount of cider was involved to ease his reluctance to talk about these events. We ended up with two pages of bullet points of the sequential events between him being at university in Budapest to arriving in England as a wounded conflict refugee, basically the events of 1956. When I first read these two pages I was fascinated and shocked but in equal measure and it went some way to explaining Dad's reluctance to speak of these events. I really knew almost nothing of these events. It is commonplace that people who have genuinely experienced the trauma of conflict and war are reluctant to speak about it. It is just too painful to recount. I'm no phycologist but maybe it is to protect loved ones from the truth and pain of conflict and the desperate desire that our own children will not have to experience it. Or is it just a kind of PTSD? I don't know. All I know is that I am very glad not to have experienced war and conflict.

Following the completion of the bullet point synopsis of Dad's escape from Hungary we really wanted more. This had wetted our appetite considerably and there had to be much more so we set about trying to persuade Dad to flesh out the bullet points with more information and recollections. He kept telling us that there wasn't much more he could say and that what we had was about it.

Further nagging from George finally persuaded Dad to try and flesh out the synopsis. This took the initial form of George taking Dad to the pub to discuss Dad's early memories of growing up in Hungary. George took copious notes and typed them up for Dad to read through and suggest additions and alterations. The sessions started to evolve and Dad started to become more interested in the project and memories came flooding back which, in turn, sparked other memories of people, places and events. Then, following an eventual enforced retirement at the age of 79, due to a stroke, Dad started to continue writing his memories down himself as he was now able to concentrate his time in that direction. He had begun to unlock memories that had been long buried and was enjoying reminiscing and piecing his life together.

There was a point when Dad started to become a little frustrated about the lack of interest the family were taking in his writing of his memoirs. This is reflected later on in the book and it wasn't a lack of interest, it was just that my siblings and I were still working full time so it wasn't always easy to find time to discuss it. His health was also slowly deteriorating which started to get him down and he had little else to concentrate on whilst the rest of us lived our very busy lives. We did try and read various chapters he had written and try and discuss, pass comment and ask questions and I certainly now regret not spending more time doing this with him, if only to give him the encouragement to continue. Despite this perceived lack of interest he did continue with the chapters which finished with his early life in England. Thank goodness he did continue.

When it came to arranging and editing the book for publication I was faced with two problems. Firstly, Dad's style of writing was as he spoke and Hungarians tend to speak sentences the wrong way around. For example a Hungarian would say "Hungarian I am" (a little like Yoda speak). I therefore had to rearranged his writing into a slightly more readable form of English but it was also very important not to make it too perfectly English so as to retain his voice. I think I have managed to retain his voice which was very important to us. A wonderful and totally unexpected pleasure of rearranging the book was that I felt that Dad was almost talking to me as I did it and this made it a very special experience so I am so glad I did it. The second problem was that there were so many sessions where Dad jumps all over the place in time and history. This was probably because one memory led to another from another time and sometimes he had forgotten he had written certain parts already. It was an arduous job to put all the sessions and chapters into some kind of sequential order and to avoid repeating things. Inevitably there are bits and pieces repeated but only to quantify the particular theme or event at the time.

After Dad's death on 31 July 2019 we were determined to finish Dad's book and publish it as a record of his life for future generations and as a suitable tribute to an unsung hero of the 1956 Hungarian Uprising. It should already be obvious to you that George and I are not professional writers, far from it, and Dad certainly wasn't but through the journey of putting this book together we have tried hard, and with love, to capture Dad's life in print as a fitting tribute to him and his extraordinary life.

The title of the book has been a difficult issue. Right from the moment Dad decided that he wanted to put his memoirs together he wanted to call it 'Have You Got Any Titpaste'. This is explained in the book and was a language misunderstanding in an English chemist when he first came to England and he was in the early days of learning English and wanted to buy tooth paste from a good looking young girl. He always thought this a very amusing little anecdote but I'm not sure we could really use it as the book title if we were to officially publish the book. You need a title that gives some kind of clue as to the subject of the book. I'm very sorry Dad, I know it was your wish, but we can't use it as the title but I thought I would mention it here.

It must be acknowleded that without the persistent and tenacious cajoling of George to get the initial two page synopsis out of Dad and then instigate the subsequent sessions and typed them up then Dad would not have eventually become interested and started writing himself and this book would never have happened. As a result we would probably be none the wiser of the majority of the content of this book which would have been lost, and regretted, forever. A massive thank you to George for all your efforts and incredible patience. Thanks also to our wonderful cousin Hugh Thomas who, as a 'real' professional published author of a biography of a WW2

RAF hero, gave us his enthusiastic advice, support and, most importantly his encouragement to see the project through. He also did some editing work and produced the excellent family tree shown in the appendix. Thanks a million Hugh, it's not to your standard but we got there in the end. Thanks also to Dad's cousin Lali (Lajos Gaal) who lives in Budapest and Dad contacted him regularly for his recollections and confirmation of his memories and I'm sure these conversations triggered other hidden, long forgotten, memories.

I think that this project did give Dad a lot of pleasure, most of the time, and gave his enforced retirement some kind of structure and meaning. He would be delighted that we have finally completed his book. We raised a glass of cider and Unicum chaser to you Dad. Cheers (egeszsegere).

Nick Solti, January 2022.

Preface - "An Excellent Suggestion"

The crossing of the Hungarian border, together with the harrowing experience I had when they tried very hard but thankfully unsuccessfully to kill me with two bullets would affect lots of people, mainly those who were probably emotionally less well balanced than I was at the time and was probably causing them nightmares. It was an experience I would never want to repeat, and I would not wish the experience on my worst enemy.

I remember lying in the darkness convinced that I was dying less than twenty-five feet from the border. I started to lose consciousness but dying did not scare me. Lying there, semi-conscious, I was still able to move my head from side to side and as I looked up, I could see a magical scene. If it was not for the deadly serious nature of the situation, it would have been beautiful. In the darkness, the search lights from the guard tower were probing around and snow began to fall. They looked like small powder puffs or pieces of candy floss, flying in the wind, and it seemed wondrous and magical when mixed with the search lights from the guard towers.

Luckily, it never gave me nightmares but there was one small part which kept haunting me for years after. While I was lying on the frozen ground, semi-conscious, amid the bedlam of noises from the machine guns and grenades I kept hearing a haunting voice from the left. A voice of a young girl, sobbing and crying, "I do not want to die, I do not want to die – please, somebody help me, I do not want to die".

This would repeat over and over again from about ten to fifteen feet away. Eventually, the volume of her voice diminished with an additional gurgling sound and, with a sigh the sound ended and I assumed that she either had fainted or died.

Chapter 1 - Early Years: Acs

I made my reluctant appearance into this world on a cold, wet and foggy Hungarian mid-November day in 1933 (18 November).

I must have been reluctant because I did not stop yelling and crying for two or three days according to my parents, Leo and Rozalia and my very disapproving six-year-old sister, Magdi, who must have realised that she now had competition for her parent's love and affection.

I was protesting against the change of my previously cozy, safe, and warm abode to this cold, noisy and frightening environment.

I must have worn myself out from yelling or may have realised that nobody took the slightest notice of my protest. According to my parents I was a 'very good baby' afterwards, whatever that meant.

We lived in a very small village called Acs (pronounced Arch), on the western edge of Hungary, some thirty miles from the Austrian border which had no resident doctor or mid-wife, so I was born in a nearby city (the second largest in Hungary) called Gyor (pronounced Duor) in the maternity unit of the hospital. There was another hospital much closer at Komarom, but it did not have a maternity unit.

My parents were typical Hungarian middle class professional people. My father was a chemical engineer and my mother, a qualified teacher who like her siblings, decided to give the profession up after my sister's birth in 1927.

My father worked at a sugar beet refinery factory, owned by an Austrian named Patzenhoffer who also owned another sugar factory in Hungary at Ercsi, where my father started his career. He had been released from the POW camp in a Siberian salt mine, where he had been held for three years during the First World War. The Patzenhoffers also owned two other sugar refineries in Austria.

My father specialised in assessing the content of sugar beet and, together with the help of an assistant, was responsible for analyzing samples of sugar and water from each batch of beet entering the factory. They were responsible for the smooth operation of the entire process, with the support from the Chief Mechanical Engineer, Erno Negro. My father was also responsible for making any innovations and improvements to the process.

Patzenoffer and Co. provided all their permanent staff with accommodation according to their status and the size of their family as part of their remuneration, which created a large private estate with all the trappings. We didn't need to leave the estate for supplies, resources, or recreation.

They also provided a gardener, who spent half of a day a week with each family, to attend to the communal and private gardens, and clear the snow from the paths in the winter. He also cut wood for our fires. His wife did our main wash every fortnight and we paid her privately for this service.

There was a house in a Swiss-style at the top of our lane, where the general manager of the factory lived with his wife. Opposite us lived the commercial manager, Josef Halzl. He was an Austrian with a Hungarian wife, and a son also called Josef. Josef was the same age as me and according to my stepmother was a "suitable" play mate for me. However, I had other ideas as he was dull, but extremely clever. Magdi sent me a cutting from a Hungarian magazine many years later reporting that he had become the CEO / Managing Director to one of the biggest Hungarian utility companies. I believe it was the Electricity Generating company.

Our apartment block in this two-story building included a basement which contained a large communal laundry area where the four families took turns to carry out their weekly wash. The rest of the basement was divided by four lockable enclosures where we could store our firewood, coal, potatoes, vegetables, wine and other useless clutter which every family routinely accumulates.

At the entrance to our block stood a giant lime tree. It may not have been that giant, but to a small boy it seemed huge. Anyhow, it was a very large tree and when it flowered it looked like somebody had emptied a small bathtub full of golden syrup all over it.

The smell was overwhelming, and my stepmother opened all the front windows wide, allowing the perfume to drift right through the house.

The bees got over exuberant, or drunk on the nectar, and their excited buzzing could be heard hundreds of feet away.

We lived on the ground floor. Opposite us lived Erno Negro, the Chief Mechanical Engineer with his wife. He was working very closely with my father on any innovations and improvements to the production of the factory.

Above them lived the Havrillay family who was the Chief Electrical Engineer, with his wife and three very young daughters. The oldest one, Marie, insisted on accompanying Josef and me, but we didn't want a girl three to four years younger to play with us. The problem was that there was nobody else for her to play with so we reluctantly put up with her tagging along.

We used to be horrid to her by running away and hiding, which often ended in tears, and this sometimes resulted in a good ticking off by our parents.

Over us lived John Weber, the firm's Chief Accountant who lived with his old, widowed, and disabled mother.

At the bottom of the lane was an area where all the tradesmen and their families lived - fitters, blacksmiths, carpenters, painters, plumbers, along with a water buffalo driver. They lived around two large quadrangles with a big stand-pipe, in the middle of which was a large grill for the disposal for wastewater since there was no internal plumbing.

They had communal lavatories and showers, and a good-sized swimming pool which, to my stepmother's annoyance, I preferred to use as it was more fun.

I had an 'unapproved friend' called Andras, the foreman carpenter's son who also lived there. He was not allowed into the senior staff swimming pool. I really enjoyed playing with Andras, but we got into quite a lot of scrapes together.

Senior management were well provided for. We had our large recreation park in a small conifer forest, which was fenced in. Each family had their own gate keys. We had a large swimming pool, a smaller one for children and another for toddlers. We had two tennis courts; one was floodlit since the heavy summer heat meant that we could only play in the evening. In the winter, the floodlit court, made of clay, was banked up all around, flooded and turned into an ice rink.

The thing I enjoyed the most was a very large slide that had wheels and could be carted from the sandpit to the swimming pool. After a good slide we would land in a lovely cool pool.

The earth from the swimming pools, along with other surplus soil was piled up to form the "rozsa-domb" (rose mound.) It was twenty-five foot high with a large rose covered gazebo with benches and tables where we sat in the summer evenings, resting from heat and cooling down in the evening breeze before going to bed.

We used this mound as our toboggan run in the winter as the area was completely flat. In our recreation park we also had a new nine-pin bowling alley and sunbathing area as well as showering and changing facilities.

At the top of our lane, still inside the factory fence, was a very large chalet for the Patzenhoffers with their own private conifer wood and tennis court. They used the house when the factory was working (usually from early September to Christmas) and in the holidays when they came down for some weeks with their only daughter, Dora, and an entourage including a governess, cook, maid and chauffeur.

I was only about four years old when my mother died.

She went to the hospital to have some kidney stones or gallstones removed. The operation was a success, but she had some infection as a result and that was before penicillin was available.

The only memory I have of my mother is when she got home from hospital. A bed had been made up for her in our sitting room so that the family could be together. I remember her lying there, very pale, and white, asking for a cup of tea. As our maid brewed it she was instructed to let me bring it to her as "it tasted so much better." She died on her 39th birthday, 1st May in 1937.

I cannot remember anything about the funeral, but my father arranged for one of his sisters, my Aunt Irma, who was Dodie's mother to come and look after us.

Aunt Irma stayed with us until my father remarried Elizabeth Kavacs in 1938. She was the daughter of a large landowner. I thought she was a rather plain woman with a narrow outlook on life and a strong obsession about discipline and etiquette, particularly about poor table manners which resulted in sharp slaps to my hand or bottom.

She was an excellent cook and very house proud, running the house with the help of a live-in maid with the precision of a military operation.

At that time in rural Hungary, it was pretty typical for women to follow this approach. A local village girl's only ambition after leaving school at sixteen was to find a husband, have children and keep the house in an exemplary manner.

As children we accepted and respected our stepmother

but she never showed any real love or affection. There was no way we could have a cuddle with her, this was "just not done". This attitude must have rubbed off on me as I am not very demonstrative in showing my feelings. I like to keep feelings private and under control.

Looking back, my life was vastly different with my mother when compared with Elizabeth. My mother loved music and as a teacher she had to play musical instrument, the Harmonium and Cimbalom. On occasions my father accompanied her on the violin which he played very, very badly!

We had one of those "very modern" early wind-up gramophones with a dozen or so records. The gramophone had a very large brass trumpet-like amplifier. The records provided a rather scratchy sound, but nonetheless, the house was always full of music.

My father was very well-read, reading books in the house and from the local lending library. He was also very keen on music. Perhaps this originated from his father (my grandfather) who worked in the Royal Opera House.

In contrast, I never saw my stepmother with any books, except perhaps a cookbook and the "Sunday Missal".

I wonder how those two managed to live with each other relatively harmoniously. At least that's how it appeared to us on the surface.

After my mother's death there was no music in the house apart from the radio on a Sunday afternoon, playing Hungarian gypsy music. My stepmother never missed that.

I know the phrase "learning on your father's knees" can be a bit of a cliché but in this case that was exactly what happened when he introduced me to stamp collecting. I remember sitting on my father knees, as I was too small to sit on the chair next to him, by his very large glass topped desk. This was his pride and joy because it was made to his own specification and design. It is still in daily use by Zsuzsa (my sister Magdi's daughter).

My father bought home lots of used envelopes, leaving them in his office, from which we cut out the stamps, soaked them off the envelopes, and dried them, sorting them out by countries and sets. We'd look for water marks and also tried to match the perforations of the stamps to a chart sheet.

I was delighted that the following year Father Christmas bought me my first stamp album together with a magnifying glass and a watermark dish. Most of the stamps were Hungarian but there were also Austrian and German stamps and stamps from other countries too. I used to ignore Austrian stamps (used in Hungary between 1851-1868, before the first Hungarian stamps were issued). These are now at a premium price (from £20-£80 each).

Acs was a very small village and the boy's school, dismal and austere, was two miles away from where we lived along with a less frightening girl's school run by nuns. Magdi and I walked to a mile and half, on an exposed road, regardless of the weather. It could be a summer heat wave or minus ten in the snow, it was the only way to get there.

The schools ran six days a week, from 8am to 1pm. On Sundays, we still had to make the same journey to church for the Sunday mass together, this time with our parents.

I was a rather small and sickly child and lost a lot of schooling as a result. My parents took me away and educated me privately. A widower from the estate, Mrs. Szabo, was an accountant, who also worked part time in the office, was allowed to keep her flat. She was a well-qualified teacher and I thought she was very good. The lessons strictly followed the school timetable (8am-1pm each week, six days a week with homework etc.). In Hungary there are just two terms, September to Christmas followed by New Year to Saint Peter / Paul day on 29th June. At the end of each term, we were examined by the Headmistress and Mother Superior of the girl's school, licensed by the Minister of Education. The lack of proper public schooling was probably because I did not have any appetite at all, barely eating, in spite of my stepmother's fantastic cooking.

One of the reasons for disliking mealtimes so much was that often, whilst in the middle of an exciting game, I was called in for lunch where I did not just have to wash my hands, but I also had to wash my face, comb my hair and change my clothes, unless they were spotless. Sometimes I was even made to have a shower before sitting down. At the table I was constantly watched, and the meal was punctuated by my stepmother's comments about my table manners (or lack of them) which she was obsessed with. As mentioned earlier, I was often reprimanded for any infringements.

The only time I really enjoyed my food was during summer when I spent three weeks at my grandparents (stepmother's parents). There, miraculously, my appetite improved as they gave me good warning of approaching mealtimes. After compulsory hand washing, we sat round a large table and were allowed to help ourselves. There were no lectures about manners. We could leave uneaten food on the plate if we'd had enough.

Not surprisingly, after each of these visits, I used to put two or three pounds on my scrawny frame.

During one of these very hot and long summer holidays I noticed a beautiful girl with long, gloriously blonde hair and a very slender, brown pair of legs showing under her short tennis skirt playing at the Patzenoffer's private court.

Immediately I fell deeply in love with her and decided that I would never marry anyone else but her. I found out later that she was Patzenhoffer's only daughter called Dora. My lovely, beautiful Dora, the only girl for me. I watched her, drooling from a distance, and was completely besotted.

Magdi had met Dora several times when she got fed up playing with her governess or wanted to play tennis doubles. Magdi and a friend were asked to make up the foursome. I could not sleep and was off my food even more than usual. Magdi noticed my love-sick behaviour and I confessed to her about Dora.

Magdi pointed out that Dora may not want to marry me and that she was also three to four years older than me. Dora could only speak German. Her Hungarian was very pitiful, and I could not speak any German at all. I believed that Magdi's objections stemmed from jealousy about my happiness, all of which could be solved once you reached the wise old age of nine.

During another long, hot summer holiday, we spent a lot of time in the swimming pool but apart from that, with the absence of modern video games and our parents too busy to play with us, we used to play 'shops'. We filled up old, discarded medicine bottles with various coloured liquids which were obtained by soaking the lining of quality envelopes which provided fantastic colours. Sometimes we scented them with flowers, mint, and lavender to fill our shop.

We also tried to sell each other small pictures and cards and other items cut out from magazines. The 'money' we used were even-sized, circular flat pebbles taken from drives or paths and we took turns to buy each other's products. Occasionally, we managed to ensnare some unsuspecting, innocent adult to buy our goods for real pennies!

The factory owned a pair of pitch-black giant water buffalos, who had a frightening pair of horns. They worked to pull the railway wagons fully loaded with some fifteen to twenty tons of sugar, all crated, bagged and sealed, to the railway sidings about a quarter of a mile away. This happened about once or twice weekly and the wagons were picked up by the next freight train heading for Vienna or Budapest to a main distribution centre, or sometimes directly to a confectionary factory.

Between those trips the water buffalos distributed coal and firewood to every family on the estate, providing two full buckets of ice a week for our fridges which were more like cool boxes. They also collected our weekly rubbish.

Apart from those tasks, they seemed to have relatively luxurious lives. They were stabled in the semi-basement below the carpenter's shops, which was warm and dry in the winter but nice and cool during the summer heat. They could get in and out of their big paddock at will, wallowing in a pond to cool down. From there, they could go to a meadow of several acres to graze.

The water buffalo driver was a large dark, rather hairy sort of chap, and a bit frightening with a very large black moustache. Perhaps he was competing with his buffalo!

I was fascinated to watch him and his team. The driver had a very long whip which was never used in anger, but gently tapped the right cheek of the buffalo which was walking on the right to turn left and touching the left-hand animal on the left cheek to turn right.

I used to know his name and his beasts, as well as the commands to go and stop but I have forgotten them. In spite of both the driver and the buffalo's fearsome appearance they were very gentle and docile.

During the 1930s in Hungary, just as now, when ladies get together for a coffee morning or afternoon tea, the subject inevitably comes up about their children's achievements, plans and ambitions for them. When roles and positions are discussed most have high intentions such as bankers or surgeons.

At one of these occasions when my stepmother had a coffee morning with four or five of her friends and neighbours, the same subject came up. As my stepmother had never asked me what I wanted to be and as I was playing nearby at the time, I was called in. She asked, "What do you want to be when you grow up?" I confidently replied at the top of my voice "I WANT TO BE A BAFFALO

DRIVER!" My stepmother nearly fainted. It was weeks before she regained her usual composure. After that I was instructed to tell her friends that I wanted to be a chemical engineer like my father. At the time, apart from film stars, bankers and politicians that was a very highly paid job in Hungary. I'm afraid I never lived up to her plans and expectations and, rather disappointingly, I ended up as a roofing contractor.

When the Russians invaded Hungary from the Ukraine, the country was already suffering from the earlier German invasion. The Soviets pursued the Germans westwards.

Everyone got very jittery about the Russians, who had a very bad reputation. Propaganda showed posters displaying drunken Russian soldiers bayoneting babies didn't help their image. Anybody with an Austrian, German, or other western heritage, was preparing to leave the country.

The German Propaganda machine swore that a new 'Maginot' Line was going to be built along the Austrian border and no Russian soldier could possibly enter Austria.

In fact, it was only going to be built in the over-imaginative, wishful mind of Mr. Goebbels. It was simply propaganda since the German army did not, at that point, have the resources.

Chapter 2 - Apprentice Arsonists

Opposite to our apartment stood a very old and dilapidated nine pin bowling alley, made from wood, with a felt roof. Next door, practically touching the bowling alley wall, stood the estate's ice store. A very large concrete underground tank, like a small swimming pool, was filled with ice slabs taken from the local lakes in the winter and stored between layers of straw. The roof was made up of a foot deep of reed, forming a thatch for insulation.

On the other side of the alley stood the firm's main sugar warehouse. When it was full there were several hundred tons of sugar ready to be bagged, boxed, and dispatched.

One dull, hot summer's day, we noticed that there were a lot of dry leaves, small twigs, and litter inside the bowling alley, swept in by the wind during the summer months. One of us had the bright idea to light a small fire. I went home to get the matches and we started a small fire. However, it got bigger and bigger, although there was probably a lot more smoke than fire. We got very frightened and two of our gang, Marie, and Joseph (the saint), legged it.

Andras and I managed to stamp out the fire, but we were photographed. We never knew who took the photograph, but we assumed it was a German secret agent. These agents were everywhere in the country. In the evening, my father, stone-faced, called me to take down his ceremonial sword from the wall, made me bend down and I got three or four sharp slaps with the flat of the sword. I had a sore bottom for at least three or four days after that. That was the only time my father ever hit me or even raised his voice to me.

It's not a great surprise that my father nearly got the sack. It was only his long, unblemished work record that saved him.

If the fire had taken hold of the main sugar store, nobody would have been able to put the blaze out. It would have destroyed half of the factory as well as half of the estate.

The Patzenhoffers owned hundreds of acres of land on the west of our estate where tenant farmers grew the sugar beet for them.

One of my father's duties was to oversee the beet production during the growing season, regularly inspecting the crops. The factory also had a light, narrow gauge railway line running from the farms to the factory which was used to bring in the beet with six or seven wagons at a time drawn by the water buffaloes.

The factory also had a hand-propelled "treszina" with a forward-facing seat, where three or four people could sit, driven by a large lever in the middle pushing it to and fro, like the handle from a modern lawnmower propelling it forward or backwards. My father was taken out by a strong young lad propelling the machine on his inspections of the farms.

During the summer weekends the senior staff were allowed to borrow this machine and go out picnicking. My stepmother made a fantastic picnic hamper and we usually finished up in our favourite spot under a large willow tree by a small river. Actually, it was more of a rivulet in the summer, a foot deep and four or five feet wide. It was, though, beautifully clear, and cool. In the winter, it was more like a small torrent which actually fed the factory's two lakes where the ice was harvested for the icehouse.

Acs had no resident doctor in the village. If we needed one, we had to call a doctor from Komarom, seven miles away, arriving in a pony and cart. I admired his transport as it was not the old-fashioned dog cart which was an all-open wooden construction. His was made of light aluminium tubes with a leather-covered seat at the front, big enough for three people with a windscreen and a canvas roof. It also ran on pneumatic tyres.

The factory was virtually self-contained. It had two main large coal-fired boilers providing all the heat, driving all the machinery. However, they had boiler problems during the year previous and so my father built a small emergency boiler, with Erno Negro.

Electricity was supplied from the main grid, but a large generator had been installed, driven by the boilers. It provided all the electricity, not just for the factory but also for the entire estate in case there was a power cut.

During the refining process, once the sugar had been boiled from the beet and allowed to crystallise, the resulting brown liquid emptied down a chute to a large perforated stainless-steel drum which spun at 10,000 revolutions per minute, forcing the mass to the inner walls of the drum and squeezing the light brown water from the sugar crystals. A jet of water was sprayed on the wall, where the brown colour become much lighter.

When the cycle finished, the centrifuge stopped spinning and the contents dropped from the drum to another chute, where it arrived at a second centrifuge. At this point the colour of the solid, after having been washed, was more like the colour of demerara. The process was repeated a third time when the colour became pure white. The solid was then dried, becoming ordinary crystal sugar, and then made into cubes.

Some of the crystal sugar, once dried, was milled to make a powder. Some was even re-milled to make icing sugar.

My father had discovered that the water used in the washing process, which was sent down into the sewers, actually contained just under 14% sugar.

With the help of Erno Negro my father managed to collect this water, pumping it back to the next batch of fermentation tanks. This increased overall sugar production by 10% or more. This method then was adapted by the other Hungarian factory at Ercsi, as well as the two Austrian factories.

As a result of this innovation there was a large celebration in the Patzenhoffers private villa where all the senior management from all the factories and their wives and guests gathered. My father was presented with a very large and very heavy solid silver Salver, (sorry about the pun!) engraved with his name. Erno Negro was also presented with a smaller one.

Our Salver was displayed in the most prominent position in our sitting room and was repeatedly shown off by my stepmother to anybody who was interested (or not!)

together with details of the presentation ceremony, such as what the ladies wore and their make-up etc.

My father's last contribution to the factory, before having to retire to Kunszenmarton for health reasons, was to purchase a steam locomotive that fitted on the narrow-gauge railway, replacing the water buffaloes, where it pulled ten to fifteen fully laden wagons to the factory, increasing the length and weight of the train by about half.

Chapter 3 - Early Days

My parents were typical Hungarians, middle class professionals. My father, Leo Karoly, had been a chemical engineer, who he had been all his life since he had left school. He went to some kind of special school although I'm not sure what and qualified and then worked the sugar beet refinery.

He visited several factories, including Ercsi and Acs, including Papsen Hoffer (Patzenhoffer) sugar factories. There were several of the factories in central Europe, two in Austria and one in Hungary. My father spoke fluent German but worked in the Ercsi and Acs factories.

During 1942, when the Russians began to invade Budapest, my family and I moved away, as did the technical staff at Papsen Hoffer, most of them travelled to Austria as they were naturally scared of the Russians.

My stepmother had brought me up since I was four. I respected and trusted her, but there was no real love for me or my sister. She was quite tyrannical, very intent on us having to follow rules and she administered beatings; holding your fork the wrong way could result in spanking. My stepmother was only like this with us, not my father. I can't remember them arguing, at least not in front of us.

Magdi became a qualified primary school teacher. Secondary school teachers needed a degree. She had been a secretary in Gyor, where my sister and I were born. She was mad on water sports, swimming and rowing in the Danube and was also a ferocious reader. For two summer holidays she had read every book in Kunsemarten, at least 500 books. Even when she was really ill, towards the end of her life, she never stopped reading. A very intelligent lady, highly knowledgeable about all subjects and well-read across a broad range of topics.

She met Frank, also born in Gyor, an engineer who worked in the same factory. They were married and Frank actually came up with an invention (something to do with hydraulic pumps as he was a hydraulic engineer.) Originally the pumps were going to be very expensive, since they came from Switzerland. To reduce some of the costs, Frank became friendly with a university professor who assisted in the calculations. Frank worked on the technical drawings. The outcome was about a quarter of the original cost and they even started to export the pumps back to Switzerland. The factory built their home for them, but unlike us, they eventually had to pay it off.

When they moved, she started teaching in Budapest and continued for thirty years until she retired. Frank carried on working at the same factory until he retired.

Before the war - life in Budapest

I personally never really lived in Budapest during this time, so my memories are brief, but I do remember it was a bustling and lively place.

As far as I can recall, life was culturally very similar to Austria; very bohemian with a pre-war cafe society that was very much all the fashion. The buildings were lovely, clean, and modern and they were as unique as those in Venice. There were big metropolitan operas, concerts, and balls that never seemed to end.

At this time my family and I were living in Kunsemarten, a rural town southeast of Budapest. Before the war I went to Budapest every year as it was en-route to various destinations. We'd take the train, stop overnight in the city, maybe visit the zoo, and carry on with our journey via rail. I was between ten and twelve years old and I have a few photos of Magdi and I at the zoo. Hardly any of the animals seemed to be caged. I wouldn't go into the Lion's den as they were loose, so I thought they'd eat me! The zoo had a very successful hippo breeding program which was the only one in the world at the time.

Invasion – living in a Nazi occupied territory

My circumstances did not change at all. At this point, Austria had been taken over by Germany. I remember that it was a Sunday morning and suddenly, before anybody had woken up, every train was full of tanks, guns, and ammunition and all the roads were full of armoured cars and German troops.

We found this out, along with everyone else, on the radio. There was no resistance from the Hungarian army as they were already allies with the Germans. I can't specifically remember the radio report; I was 14 years old.

Nothing at that time happened to our family, everything seemed normal. As we were living in Kunsemarten, in the Hungarian countryside, we never saw a German soldier. The only indication that our country had been invaded was through newspapers, which were mostly all propaganda and The Signal magazine which told how wonderful the Germans were, showing pictures of politicians shaking hands.

The Hungarian government were still in power but were merely figureheads. Admiral Miklos Horty was portrayed as our leader. In fact, Berlin made the orders.

This was a volatile time for Hungary, already overrun by the German troops but this was not the only threat. Russia was also threatening, pushing at the Hungarian borders.

By the end of the war, the Russians, threatening the borders for so long, began to push the Germans back. They were only halted, temporarily as it happened, by the Danube. At least two-thirds Budapest lay in ruins, far worse than the pictures of the London Blitz from 1940. Most of the bridges had been blown up by the Germans to stop the Russians. For the latter part of the war the Russians encircled the city, and it was under siege for eight months.

My father had many relatives in Budapest. Because of the siege they were starving to death, so we took food and other supplies to them. My father and I travelled by train and took as much as we could carry. I thought it was quite an adventure. We became stuck there for two months, staying with one of my father's relatives. I was twelve at the end of the war and it was during the winter. We weren't uncomfortable as we stayed with relatives. We had beds and everything we needed but lacked food. We had running water and cooked on gas.

Things were so bad that we headed out with carving knives into the freezing cold looking for dead horses in the streets, slicing them up and taking the meat back for cooking. Horses littered the streets and were used for everything. If a horse was killed during the evening there was unlikely to be anything left by the morning. People stripped the carcass bare as soon as possible. It was miserable, but after two months the Russians pushed through, and my father and I were able to leave.

Both German and Russian troops had succeeded in destroying Budapest but, in fact, most of the damage was carried out by the United States Air Force carpet-bombing the city night and day.

What's in a name: from Schmelka to Solti

By 1942/3 Hungary was closely allied to the Germans, although not yet occupied. Middle-class Hungarians were very much against this. As a political gesture, thousands, and thousands of Hungarians with Austrian or German names changed them as a protest against the imminent occupation. It was a silent political protest. My father decided to follow suit. There was a list of Hungarian names he could choose from. He decided on Solti. I had been very close to my father but after changing our names, which seemed very unnecessary, we had a big argument and fell out. What was rather sad was that we never talked to each other again. We did, however, continue to keep in contact by letter but it was the end of our close relationship.

The change of surname impacted severely on my family. They never forgave my father for changing our surname. I visited my grandmother just once more and she was frosty and barely wanted to see me because of the rift between me and my father. We'd write the odd letter, perhaps, but I never have the same relationships as I'd had before. I never saw my grandfather at all, who had been a lighting engineer at the Royal Opera House and had become deaf from the numerous orchestras he'd had to endure

Russian invasion

We had managed to escape Budapest because the Russians were pushing back the Germans troops. When we got back to Kunszenmarton there was a lot of fighting. The Germans succeeded in destroying the only bridge over the river Koros and were using Hungarians as 'rear guards' as they retreated.

One day, when we were back home, there was a knock at the window of our house. Two Hungarian soldiers stopped by asking for some water. We began to talk to them as we were getting the water. They hadn't eaten for two days and said they were going to move out of Kunszenmarton the next day and fall back. As they were talking, they were shot at by a Russian sniper, who missed them. They managed to get away with some bread and water and left under darkness that night. When I returned to Kunszenmarton a few years ago the bullet holes from the sniper were still visible in the wall, although they been filled in with some plaster.

There was no real difference between the Germans and the Russians. They were generally the same in terms of daily contact, but the key difference was that the Germans behaved a little more gentlemanly. The Russians, however, were ignorant. There were times when they didn't even know which country they had invaded!

Things were not great either way. Once the Russians had control of Hungary, they held an 'election', which was a farce but purely for show, enabling them to take full control legally.

They were now able to do precisely what they wanted. The first thing they did was to make a law that all land was taken over by the state, along with everything on and in it. Landowners were classed as 'kulaks' so effectively an enemy of the state. My father had bought some land, about 80 hectares, prior to the war. He owned a farm and buildings which were confiscated. The family (Lajosh) vineyard was also confiscated at that time, but my father bought about a quarter of it back after the war was over. The Russians just walked in and kicked everyone out.

The Russians came through, going from house to house, drunken, looting and looking for 'Zsaka' (women). Wives and daughters weren't safe. My sister Magdi was eighteen and my Mum made her up so that she looked like a really horrible old lady. A few Russians tried to take her and my father tried to stop them. Our dog (a German shepherd) attacked them. They killed the dog but ran way. My sister was safe.

There was to be no escape. When I had gone to University in Budapest my stepmother was kicked out of the family house and was allocated a single room in someone else's. Our house was deemed 'too big for her' and given to another Communist. My father had died by this time.

While it was true that the Germans had confiscated property, they only took property relating to industry such as factories, not homes. It didn't affect us quite as much.

Chapter 4 – Living Under The Communist Regime

We did not notice any immediate change in our daily life from the regime change. The first blow we suffered after six months or so was the official notification from the Rakosi government that our farmhouse and our land had been confiscated and the ownership had been transferred to our tenant, who was actually living and working on the land.

We were classed as 'Kulak' (the absentee landowners) who "do not deserve to profit from the peasants' "sweat and labour," according to the communists. We were actually "compensated" in the 1980's and my sister and I had to share the compensation of some £300. This was the equivalent of about two farthings in the pound. Even this money came with a caveat; we had to declare that by accepting this money we would never make any further claims on it.

We settled down to our everyday problems of the shortage of virtually everything. I mentioned earlier that the withdrawing Germans had emptied out all stocks from the warehouses and the manufacturing of replacements had just started up.

Some brainy chap once said, "Necessity is the mother of all inventions". We had to improvise and recycle everything. If a window glass got broken, we would try to fix it with some old and forgotten cold frame covers with rotten timber frames. We took out the glass from the frames and, using my mother's diamond ring, we would cut the glass to replace the broken pane.

We also made our own putty. I remember we mixed linseed oil with something that looked like talcum powder (I have no idea where we got that) to make our putty.

We used large timber packing cases in our loft. Taking them carefully apart to use the timber to make repairs to the fence, which needed mending, including the carefully extracted of the nails which would then have to be straightened. No nails of any sort were available in the shops.

We made our own tabletop, charcoal, two-ring cooker using old bricks, clay and some old iron rods. The charcoal was still available in the villages. As matches were extremely scarce, we tried to light our fires and candles by harvesting the heads of reeds, which grew at the riverbank. This was dried, then mixed with sulphur from the chemist and with a flint and steel we managed to produce some sparks. After many attempts and a few curses, eventually we started the sulphur-infused wad to smoke and after a lot of huffing and puffing we managed to light a small piece of paper, our candles, and fires.

At the time, we got electricity in the house but apart from lighting and a small worktop-sized single ring stove, everything including cooking, heating etc. was done by wood and coal fires.

The electricity supply was unpredictable and spasmodic. Candles were no longer available in shops, so we were forced to make our own candles. We made them from rolled up cardboard to form a tube and a good quality string, which had previously been soaked in wax for the wick. Standing them upright in a bucket of sand we grouped them together six at the time. We then melted down all old candle stubs, carefully collected the drips, adding new bees wax from the local beekeeper, heating it up and pouring it into these tubes. This made a passable candle.

We were forced to make our soap by collecting up all fat, bacon rinds and oil and boiling it with caustic soda. This made quite a good soap for washing clothes. It was too rough for toilet soap, but I cannot remember how we overcame this problem. We made toilet paper by cutting up and folding newspaper to fit the toilet paper dispenser.

The most interesting invention we attempted was trying to make our own sugar. It was quite easy to get hold of sugar beet. Under my father's supervision we washed and shredded it and then boiled them until it was completely cooked. The problem was how to separate the sugar crystals from the watery brown liquid. A centrifuge to do this, funnily enough, was not available.

My father, with the local blacksmith / handyman, made a light steel-perforated drum lined inside with a heavy-duty material (like curtain material) using some simple gearing, attached to the back wheel of a bicycle. By peddling furiously, we managed to produce a brown sugar, similar to Demerara, which was then dried in the sun.

This contraption was "sub-let" in exchange for bee's wax or charcoal as money had become completely useless and everything had to be bartered for.

We endured 1945 /46, which was the world's worst hyperinflation. This famous, or rather infamous, world record stayed until 2008 when the Zimbabwean inflation crisis topped the Hungarian one, we experienced.

This inflation was caused by several factors. The country had just started working after the war years and the government's expenditure, mainly the salaries of all civil servants, doctors' nurses, teachers, police, and army was much bigger than the taxes collected.

Perhaps the most damaging part was the retreating German army which had looted all the gold bullion form the Hungarian national bank vaults. Paper money had no value without a gold backing and no other country would lend us any money. As a consequence, the government had to print worthless money.

This inflation was nearing 41,900 million %. The prices doubled up in the shops every fifteen hours. At the height of the inflation, if a man took home a monthly salary, he needed a large holdall or briefcase to carry it in.

That day, he could buy a month's supply of groceries for the family and pay the rent and utilities. Forty-eight hours later, the same money would only buy two dozen eggs. From then on, all salaries were paid weekly on a Friday and food shops stayed open until midnight.

An excellent example of this was that a price of a standard one-kilo loaf of bread was:

1945 - August = 6 Pengo (main currency since 1926)

October = 27P

Early November = 80P

Late November = 135P

Early December = 310P

Late December = 550P

1946 - Early January = 700P

Late January = 7000P

Early May = 800000P

Late May = 360000000P

June = 5850000000P (585 Billion)

People were unable to pronounce the millions, billions, and trillions so they were simply identified by colours. For example, one priced an article as five yellow and two blues. If one dropped a note with a low value, people just didn't bother to pick them up.

I remember seeing a magazine picture in a city. The road sweepers were cleaning up piles of discarded, wind-swept bank notes.

To the stamp collector, it was a very interesting period as the government tried to print higher value stamps but were unable to keep up with the pace of the raging inflation, so they were overprinting the existing stamps with the new values.

They invented "Ado Pengo" which meant tax pengo.

I am not sure how it was supposed to work but obviously, it did not.

The stamp collectors got over a dozen sets of very nice and colourful stamps. The government then overprinted these stamps with letters: EG: Cs 1kg i.e.: one kilogram parcel (Csomag meant parcel) and also Aj - which mean Ajalnott / registered. Heji = local. The same stamps could be used even if the price trebled up.

Not unlike our 1st and 2nd class stamps of today, where the stamps are the same, but you pay a lot more for it as the postal rate goes up.

I got in my stamp collection an envelope of a registered letter, which had one of ten thousand stamps value, one of 30,000 and one of 20,000 making a total of 60,000 Pengo to send a registered letter.

In August 1946, the Forint arrived. One could buy 1 Forint for 400 billion Pengo.

After arranging all the gardens in Kunszenmarton and establishing all the trees or espaliers, my father got rather bored with his retirement. All his life he liked to be active and very busy, and this trend was passed onto my sister and me, then from us onto our children and grandchildren. All of them managed to get good jobs and build a respectful life for their families through hard work and reliability. We are extremely proud of them all (apart from George who is mostly useless, ha ha ha).

Perhaps the only exception was Joshua who appeared to be rather laid back or even lazy. He had difficulty getting up in the morning and during our walks, he was always at the back, until we learnt that he was struggling with type 1 diabetes at the age of ten. Later, he learnt to live with this ailment with regular medication, managed to get a good job and has since been promoted so had already at a young age proved himself more useful and worthwhile.

My father managed to get a part time job at a small local factory producing edible oils, pressed from sunflower seeds but also pressing inedible seeds such as linseed. This firm, owned by a man of Polish extraction called Jankowich. The firm, as arranged, paid half of my father's salary in oil. Due to the devastating hyperinflation, it had an excellent "barter value".

I remember one incident when two or three other boys and I needed extra lessons in Latin, which was my weakest subject. The Latin teacher, Mr. Kedves (that translates to "Darling") gave us lessons and I remember carrying a gallon demijohn full of sunflower oil to him as my tuition fee. I do not remember exactly how the other boys paid, except one whose father had a smallholding and once brought in a live chicken or a basket of eggs.

I also remember that the same teacher came to our house several times, and being a bachelor, was very interested in my sister Magdi but she didn't seem to reciprocate his advantages and it all fizzled out.

Looking back on my earlier life, I realised that I never actually had, until later in my life, "real" friends. I had lots and lots of mates, but not one of those close and long-lasting friendship where one could, without hesitation, discuss one's feelings or affairs and not mind if you wanted to unburden yourself.

This is perhaps because the age difference between

myself and my sister. I was a shy and lonely boy, like an only child. I learnt to be happy or not too unhappy with my own company and keep my thoughts, plans and fears to myself and button it all up in my mind.

In the grammar school or University, I did not really make any real friends. At the secondary school, I had a classmate named Rebely with whom I used to go swimming, cinema, and dancing and later when I started flying, he also joined the club. Apart from these activities, we did not share anything else particularly personal or important to that time of a teenager's life except talk of GIRLS.

That brings me back to the topic of starting my gliding activities. I cannot recollect the exact reason why I was fascinated with any kind of flying throughout my life. I remember I became very interested in model making airplanes (the flying type). There was a model making club on Saturday afternoons at the school, which was the only time we could catch the late train home which didn't get me to bed until about 10 or 10:30. That was much too later if the next morning you had to get up at 5am to catch the train to school.

We started making small crafts with about 1ft wingspan gliders using light 3ply wood from which we had to cut out the wing profile of various sizes using balsa wood rods and then use thin string, glue and stretched grease proof like paper we made our models.

My biggest one had about a 5ft wingspan and when they were created, after six to seven weeks of work, we went to the small hill by the edge of the town and watched them perform (or not), see how they landed or crashed and then carried out first aid on the gliders before starting again and re-launch.

We also made microlights (a very small indoor powered craft) with a very fine balsa wood section. For a small fee we could buy the plans/drawing and propellers for the planes. These micro lights were powered by winding the propellers backwards, which were attached to very strong rubber bands and would provide about twenty to thirty seconds of powered flight at which point the plane would glide and, theoretically, land. We used the school's double staircase to launch these planes.

When I reached the age of sixteen, I could start gliding after a rather rigorous health check, which had to be repeated every six months. This was all recorded in our logbooks.

At Szentes there was a small airfield with a large concrete hanger, which I believe was built at the very beginning of the war but had never been used during the war. The clubhouse, a two-story building where the hanger master lived downstairs and upstairs, was an office for the duty-flying instructor and a dorm with eight beds.

We sometimes stayed there on a Saturday night as flying started at 7am the following day and we could not get there by that time if we went home. The whole building was unheated and staying there in the winter, under several layers of army blankets, which were as stiff as hardboard, was hard going. The next morning, after a freezing night's sleep, we managed to make cups of tea by plugging into a light circuit using a Heath Robinson homemade immersion heater which blew the fuse many, many times. In the summer months, it worked well.

As I mentioned earlier, the hanger master lived downstairs as he was a bachelor, and the flying instructor would come in when flying was in progress.

The gliders were old fashioned, thin plywood with canvas stretched over wings and heavily varnished. The most basic glider was called "Tucsok" (grasshopper) consisting of a single seat on the skid with a wing, fuselage, joystick and peddles but no instruments.

I was extremely lucky, as all pilots (even the jet pilots) carefully log not only airtime but also how many craft types they had flown, as well as the number of airfields they had flown from. Szentes airfield had the very last Tucsok. They never made another one.

It was replaced by a "Vocsok" (grebe), a sturdier craft with a semi-enclosed cockpit which also had three basic instruments, air speed, height, and variometer.

The gliders were launched by a winch, which was about a thousand metres away. It was a heavy tractor-like contraption with a heavy drum, onto which the stainless-steel cable was wound up, pulling the gliders to the required heights. A communication between a launch site and a winch was made by a signal by a red flag at each end. One circle with a flag is a very shallow flight for beginners. Two circles were for the more advanced and the three circles launched the pilots to the full height of 800 feet. Each signal has to be acknowledged from the winch site before the launch could take place.

The more advanced "Lepke" (butterfly), which was enclosed, and wind shielded but still open cockpit. Then there was the "Szello" (breeze), with a larger instrument panel including height and speed indictors etc. The "Pilis" (small mountain range in transodanubia) was a more sophisticated craft for the advanced pilot and had the usual instruments but also a compass for long-range flights and a turn indicator to be able to fly blind in the clouds.

There were also two-seater gliders, the older one was the "Cimbora" (friend) with seats behind each other and an open cockpit. The most upgraded version was the "Koma" (mate) with seats side by side and a totally enclosed cockpit. There was also the (thinker) "Cinke".

I had flown all the types of crafts, clocking up 72 flights with 8 hours and 22 minutes airtime. On the dual control flights, I clocked up 186 solo flights at 15 hrs and 52 mins. The total was 24hrs and 14 minutes altogether.

Life in Kunszenmarton was grinding on with the struggles which was mainly trying to cope with not being able to obtain all the goods and the constant recycling. Scarves and pullovers were taken apart and re-knitted to make new clothes. Some of my father's suits were taken apart and I got a new suit remade out of them as I had grown out of the old one made by a local tailor. In those days, due to the lack of new fabric, many things were made from old wool.

My step grandparents had about 100 angoras (white rabbits), with a few greys and blacks. The rabbits were housed in a multi-story hutch of individual cages. This would be taken to pieces section by section. The rear was covered with chicken wire, so the droppings and urine fell through and was collected by a tray below it. They were looked after by my stepmother and by my two step aunts, who watered and fed them every night. Two or three times a year they were sheared when their wool (fur) got long enough. This was then spun on a spinning wheel and the wool was used to knit garments or used as a "barter currency".

When the rabbits got too old, I'm afraid they were killed and eaten.

As a schoolboy during the summer holidays, I helped with the care of these rabbits. I was even able to spin some yarn, even if it wasn't that smooth or even.

As I mentioned earlier, everything was knitted at the time. When I wore out my swimming trunks my stepmother knitted me a new grey pair of trunks and my sister got a nice white swimsuit. Magdi begged her to knit her a bikini but was refused as it was considered 'not decent'.

My first (and last) use of these trunks turned out to be a complete disaster. I dived into the Koros (the local river) and as soon as I reached the water I felt that my soaked, knitted wool trunks had slid off me. I tried to retrieve them, but the river was quite fast flowing and silty and I could not find them. One of my mates tried to locate them as well!

By then it was late afternoon. There was a floating pontoon in the river which we used as a sunbathing platform, and which also had a diving board. The swimmers began to leave the area and all I could do was wait until dark to get home. I was getting very cold, immersed up to my neck in water. Finally, I left the safety of the pontoon to retrieve my towel from the bank with an army of vicious mosquitos. Luckily, it was still pretty warm at that time of the year and at about after 8pm I sneaked home, avoiding parts of the village, wearing a very small towel around my middle.

My stepmother was also getting rather anxious as I should have been home about four hours earlier and was about to send out the maid to look for me when I finally turned up. I never remember how my sister got on with her knitted swimsuit. After that incident, my swimming trunks were made from old curtain lining, which was found in an old and forgotten trunk, lurking in the darkest corner of our loft.

It was a family ritual that each year, after the school closed for the summer holiday, my hair was crew cut and it had a chance to grow by the time the new school year had started. The reason for this was that my father was bald as the result of my grandfather's insistence that the hair to be wetted down to your scalp so not a single strand would stay upright. Walking to the school in the mornings, sometimes in minus ten degrees temperature, without a hat, was asking for trouble in later years. My only other uncle who I met, Otto, was also completely bald. My father tried to strengthen my hair and this treatment obviously worked well.

There was another yearly ritual in the village. Four or five of us would walk upstream of the local river Koros through a thick willow planation on the flood plain which was planted to slow down the river when it was in full flow (stop flooding). We walked up some two miles or so to the railway bridge and then swam back to the village bridge. We finished this ritual by climbing down to the shoulders of the supporting bridge pillars and dive, or jump, into the river some thirty foot down.

One year, when there was a drought and the Koros was very low, we were horrified to see that at the place where we normally jumped, was only a few feet away from some very nasty and jagged steel support members, which had been cut away and never cleared up when the bridge was previously repaired. After that, this part of our yearly venture was discontinued.

Life carried on with various hiccups and problems, but the next very serious part of our life was that my father went into hospital for some operational treatment on his eyes. When he got home a week or so later, just before Easter he started to complain about pain in his left leg. Shortly after, this leg started to swell which later turned red and blue and the pain increased significantly.

We called the doctor but, because it was Easter week, he did not turn up immediately. When he eventually arrived, he diagnosed the problem of my father having thrombosis which perhaps attributed to the blood thinning and vein-expanding drugs used for procedures to his eyes. He died of Thrombosis on the 7th April 1947, one day before Easter Sunday.

The shock of my young life

The loss of my father, when I was only thirteen years old, was devastating enough. However, after we buried him and we were still in the cemetery, my stepmother went up to Lajos Gaal (my godfather) and asked, "when would you like to take the children?" Lajos Gaal and the entire funeral party, friends, and neighbours were completely speechless that after over ten years of marriage to my father she wanted to dump my sister and I like unwanted baggage as soon as possible.

I was perhaps the most shocked as I was under the illusion that she actually loved me, being the baby of the family. I was never actually able to forgive her for this act.

It wasn't just the Gaal family who would not talk to her but several others at the funeral, even those who were not present but were "reliably" informed. The main village gossipers had a field day on the subject for weeks and weeks.

With my stepmother's attempt to get rid of her "baggage" she would have been a rather well-to-do widow, with her own home and a state widow's pension and half of my father's rather generous pension too.

If my stepmother met the Gaal family a polite "good evening" or "good morning" was muttered but apart from that there was no communication at all. We, the children, kept meeting with my cousins Lali and Babus, catching the same train and attending the same classes all through the secondary school years with Babus. It would have been impossible for us not to see each other.

I was very friendly with Babus as we grew up together. When we met in Budapest when I was at university we went swimming, to parties and to concerts and dances.

The previous cool temperature at home had now turned defiantly frosty, which mainly affected Magdi as my stepmother tried to make her a second servant as we already had a live-in maid.

My sister, after finishing her schooling, could not wait to get away and immediately after she reached the age of eighteen. Eighteen was, at the time in Hungary, considered becoming an adult. She packed a suitcase and took her saved up pocket money, including mine which she borrowed (and paid back to me several times over since) and went back to Gyor.

My stepmother would not give a penny, in spite of my father's very good pension she received.

Looking back at the money, Magdi got just enough to cover the train fare, which at the time was quite reasonable. It also just covered rent for one month in a single room. She took a part-time crash course in secretarial work and got a part time job as an office junior with Frank Simon. He worked as an engineer at Gyor's biggest factory called "Vagon Gyar" which made all types of railways rolling stock from cattle trucks to passenger carriages.

Magdi and Frank worked very well together and started a deep friendship which developed much further. In 1952 they got married in the face of my stepmother's fierce opposition. Frank was eight years older than my sister. In August 1956, Zsuza was born in Gyor. Oddly enough, this was in the same hospital as I was born in and saw the daylight for the first time.

The summer before they got married my sister asked me to join her for a fortnight's summer holiday in her room. The window looked out on the "Raba", a small river and just round the corner from the Carmelite church.

A funny episode that happened during this time springs to mind:

These days all over the world, somebody tries to fleece some unsuspecting person of their money or possessions. This is not a new phenomenon and in 1949/1950 in Hungary I must admit a rather clever scam happened. The factory where Magdi and Frank worked had a very large carpenter / joiners department to finish off the interiors panelling and seating using good quality timbers.

When the shop was not very busy, they filled in their time to make anything that was usable and sellable. One of these items was to make wooden wheelbarrows. Every Saturday, when the factory only worked one shift, one of the employers clocked in at the gate with his lunchbox and clothing in a wheelbarrow. It was recorded at the gate that he booked in as a man with his wheelbarrow. Clocking out, the same thing was recorded. This was going on for some years and the scam was only discovered when someone noticed an advert to buy any old wheelbarrows. After that, some suspicious person informed the police and when they raided his premises, they found over a hundred brand new wheelbarrows were waiting to be sold. He was arrested and spent some time behind bars for this dodgy scam.

At Szentes I was finished with my secondary school education with my matriculation (a French style Baccalaureate.) We had to pass written and aural examinations in seven subjects to be able to apply for a university place.

The following day after passing matriculation everybody who planned to go to university had to return to school to fill out application forms for the university places. Unfortunately, the school would not offer any help or assistance in higher education, so most of us were completely unsure and unprepared.

I knew I wanted to be an architect as in all my life I was rather interested in the modern and ancient buildings and building methods, symmetries, proportions, and balances. My second choice was meteorology, after years of gliding when the weather is the most critical factor, as well as being fascinated by cloud formations and such like.

When I was called up to the technical university of Budapest to sit the entry exam everything went exceptionally well except my free hand drawing. For example, they projected on a large screen in front of us images like the Notre Dame in Paris and, after looking at it for two or three minutes, we were then expected to draw it with all the relevant proportions etc. Unfortunately, my drawing was not up to standard and consequently I was not offered a place on the course.

My second choice of meteorology at the Eotvos Lorand Tudomany Egyetam (the Science University with a natural sciences faculty) offered me a place. The university was named after a Nobel Prize winning university professor who discovered the famous Eotvos Inga (Eotvos Pendulum (something to do with demonstrating and measuring the gravitational fields and forces of the earth).

Each summer holiday was eight weeks because of longer school days, which consisted of six-day weeks and no half terms with a couple of holidays. I usually worked a summer job since I was fifteen years old, buying replacement clothes for the worn out / grown out of garments, or buying the necessary school equipment and stationery. The schools in Hungary did not provide any of these items apart from chalk and sponge used on the blackboards.

The only jobs I could get, while in secondary school in Szentes, was labouring on building sites. Officially, you needed to be sixteen but if you looked fit enough, they did not bother to dwell on your age.

Over two summers, I was employed as a labourer on a building site of a very large army barracks. The first year I was attached to the concreting section. Two of us had to carry tons and tons of concrete on a stretcher-like contraption from the mixing plant to the buildings to lay the foundations. All the buildings (over a dozen or so) were known as building A /B/C etc. We were carrying these concrete batches (each load was about two buckets of concrete) for eight hours a day with only a twenty-minute break. After the first shift, I was so tired that I was hardly able to walk home to my favourite Aunt, Maria, where I stayed during the work. Obviously, my muscles were toned to sit in the classroom with odd swim and athletics or walks, but not for this backbreaking labouring job.

After my first shift, with blistered hands and aching muscles, I would get home and my aunt would have a meal waiting for me as they would have already eaten and gone to bed by that time. I sat down to eat it as I was always starving. My uncle Lajos got up in the night to use the loo and seeing the kitchen light still on went on to investigate. He found me slumped on the table with food next to me untouched. I do not remember how I managed to go to work the next day but by the end of the week I still found it very hard but more manageable.

Building a nuclear bunker

The buildings had large three-story blocks for the soldiers and two stories for the officers. They all had the mess halls, kitchens, shower blocks, fuel dumps and right in the corner was the ammunition store.

It intrigued me why building 'E' had the deepest foundation and had to have very heavy reinforced bars within the floors and the walls had four-foot-deep reinforced concrete with several very large cast iron pipes sticking out of it.

During construction, all buildings were referred to as officers mess, storerooms etc. etc. but the only construction with no name was building 'E'.

When I returned to the same site early next summer I was employed as a scaffolder's mate, carrying hundreds of planks and tubes to various sites for the bricklayers to use.

It was very interesting to see that building 'E' had completely disappeared and in its place was a very large mound of earth and debris which had come out of different trenches. It was all beautifully laid out with shrubs and slabs and on the top was the biggest Russian tank I had ever seen. Only now, I realised that building 'E' must have been a nuclear bunker. We knew the barracks housed the second biggest (other than the one near Budapest) Russian tank regiment. In its' heyday they were also the home of nearly a hundred Russian tanks and armoured vehicles with all their crews and personnel.

We heard that when the tank regiment eventually withdrew back to Russia, they stripped off all moveable items from the buildings, even taps, door handles, light fittings, and urinals. All that remained were the walls and ceilings and the unwanted giant tank to remind the Hungarians of the Russians' unwanted and over-welcome stay. The tank that was left behind was an IS-2.

At the time, I was working as a Scaffolder's mate night shift (9pm to 5am) so I did not have to endure the blazing sun each day. When I got home at 5:30am I would have a quick shower and breakfast and it was then very difficult to try to sleep in the heat of the day with the curtains drawn and daytime noise making it even harder.

The remuneration for the labouring, trying to translate our wages today in England, I come up with the figure of £1 (max) a day, £6 for a full week's work. At the time in Hungary the normal working week was roughly five and a half days.

It is interesting to compare today's working practices where health and safety issues rules all our daily lives to that in 1950's Hungary.

Working on the building site, you would never see a safety barrier, untied ladders and zero safety notices. Concreting was performed in sandals and no gloves or protective headgear was used or offered and I would get dozens of blisters. Funnily enough, the days of working there with all the bruises and blisters, I do not remember a single accident happening on site.

In Kunszentmarton in the early 1950's, the local communist authority billeted in our large dining room a couple who with hundreds of others, were deported from Budapest and dumped to various villages in the country. Their 'crime' was 'undesirable elite of our previous life' but

I believe the main reason was that they all had large apartments, which were then given to top Russian army officers and their families or high-ranking communist party leaders. The apartments were sometimes divided into two or three living areas as there was a chronic shortage of liveable accommodation and the rebuilding of the city was only a quarter complete. In our house was placed a lovely, retired couple, the male was a retired colonel of the Hungarian army and his lovely wife (Babs). I cannot remember what I called him, but we had many interesting talks about his life in the army.

I was particularly interested in his story that as a young officer he took part in the 1936 Berlin Olympics, representing Hungary in the fencing (sabre) but having a nasty cold at the time he was not allowed to take even an aspirin, so he came fourth, just missing the bronze. I wonder if my fascination for fencing perhaps may have originated from this point.

One of these deported families to end up in Kunszentmarton had a son called Buba. He was good with his hands and was allocated a job to rebuild a very large chimney on the Matray brick factory, which was damaged during the war and had to be demolished and rebuilt before the factory could start producing bricks again.

During their stay, Buba, who was a very handsome young man, met Babus and they fell in love. When the deported families finally departed back to Budapest, he did not go with them. He stayed on and later, in about 1953 / 54, they got married. Lali and I were the best men at the wedding. Sometime later, they moved up to Budapest were Buba started a small building firm and Babus took a crash course in book-keeping and accounting. Later she became the chief accountant for a large firm in Budapest.

They bought a very nice house in Torokbalint, which was a small village some six to seven miles from the capital, where Buba still lives after Babus' death. As I mentioned earlier, when you are fifteen to twenty everyone loves going out and I was no exception. I had a number of very serious love affairs all of which lasted a least a week or even three. A couple of times I double-dated girls and when I was found out I finished up with a slapped face and both girls walked out on me.

As a male "chauvinistic pig" (now repentant and reformed) I thought it was very unfair to receive this treatment from them.

Now it was time to move to Budapest to attend my university course in Meteorology.

England vs Hungary: flowers and footballs

I won a competition in our parachute club, along with a girl and another boy. Our prize was to parachute into Budapest Stadium, the girl carrying flowers, we, the boys, carrying footballs, to huge cheers.

We clambered into our gear and climbed aboard the aircraft. As we approached the stadium, we prepared to make the drop, collecting our flowers and footballs, anticipating the moment when we would jump. Unfortunately, the meteorologist aboard the flight aborted our jump as the wind had increased and he was worried that we'd be blown off course, far from our target in the stadium.

Although we didn't get to drop, not all was lost. We landed soon after and managed to arrive at the stadium to watch the last ten minutes of the game. It was memorable since Hungary beat England.

(Historical note: This game was played on 23 May 1954 at the Nepstadion in front of a crowd of 92,000 and was the return fixture of the game played at Wembley on 25 November 1953 which Hungary won 3-6. Hungary also won this return fixture 7-1 with their national hero Ferenc Puskas scoring twice. At the time Hungary were ranked the number one side in the world and were also Olympic Champions at the 1952 Helsinki games. Leo was always slightly annoyed that Hungary lost the 1954 world cup final to West Germany, having been the out and out favourites and having easily beaten West Germany in an earlier round).

Careers in a Communist country – walls have ears

All my life, I'd had a fascination with buildings and how they were constructed, bricklaying, building, architecture; you name it; I loved it. No-one in particular inspired or encouraged me. It must have been something organic. I set my sights on becoming an architect and all went well until I had a practical freehand drawing exam. The problem was that my freehand skills just weren't good enough to be an architect and I didn't and couldn't progress any further.

I had to reconsider my career. My second choice was a career in meteorology, since I loved gliding and felt that it was indirectly linked to meteorology in its widest sense. It seemed to make sense at the time.

Meteorology required advanced mathematics, but

unfortunately, was well beyond my capability. After struggling for three years, I decided to call it quits. Instead, I decided to focus on structural engineering which was indirectly connected to my first love of construction, something I really enjoyed.

In 1955 I was at university in Budapest, but I never finished my degree as I lost my scholarship. I couldn't keep my big mouth shut. Someone had overheard me saying something anti-political or anti-communist against the soviet controlled authorities and reported me. A month or so later, I went to the University Treasury Department to get my monthly grant and was told that I was no longer being supported to complete my degree. They told me my scholarship had been withdrawn because of my 'anti-communist attitude.'

Of course, I had broken the golden rule of Communism, I had questioned the authorities, something that was not to be tolerated. That was it. I wasn't on speaking-terms with my father and my stepmother couldn't support me. I had to get a job as there was still a year and a half to go to complete.

Chapter 5 - Budapest

In September 1952, I moved up to Budapest to attend my university, the Eotvos Lorand University of Science at the meteorological faculty. We were housed at number 20, Maria Street, some 15-20 minutes' walk from the university.

The building was a typical, Hungarian, inner city building, four stories high. Only the front elevation was visible from the street, and it was built around a large, central courtyard. It had one large, solid, wooden double gate and inside a lockable wrought iron gate.

The rooms or apartments have only one open aspect towards the courtyard and accessed by a balcony with a wrought iron railing around on all four sides at the upper levels. The building was hemmed in with a similar design on either side, and on the back which was fantastic from a thermal insulation point of view as it had only a one or two inch gap between the buildings (to stop transmission of structural born sound transmission from one to the other).

This design was so popular in all big Hungarian cities that they were used mainly in apartment blocks but also in hotels and even offices and in those cases the building would rise to six or seven stories.

A central courtyard used by children to run around but some would have a tree, some with rockeries or water features in a corner. In those that were used as offices also had a glass roof, carpeted and with air conditioning and used as a conference centre.

Those which were used as hotels also had glass roofs. The main dining area in the courtyard was decorated with potted trees and shrubs and orchestra stand in the corner.

The sizes of the rooms or apartments depended on the size of the central courtyard. Normally, each side of the quadrangle would house between 10-15 apartments. The most desirable ones and most expensive were the front ones with the double aspect and the corner ones that were facing south were slightly bigger. Each of these buildings had a porter, janitor or custodian who looked after the gate which would be locked at night, and he would also keep the courtyard clean, swept and washed all balconies and stairs including clearing the snow from public areas too.

The Janitor's job included collecting and disposing all the rubbish each week, but the job was made easier when rubbish chutes were introduced.

The caretaker got a salary from the owner or landlord and a free apartment by the gate. He was usually a handyman and could make extra cash by providing small services like mending fuses, unblocking sinks and his wife would iron or babysit. As mentioned earlier, the gates were normally locked at night and of course, each tenant or owner had their own keys, but any visitor would not be admitted unless the caretaker contacted the owner of the apartment by intercom. This was a fantastic security system as it reduced any burglaries, robberies, or unwanted callers.

This design of the building also had drawbacks. Firstly, noise was an issue. The enclosed courtyard could get very noisy with children playing, babies crying and loud music playing and inevitable noisy neighbours which was solved by sending the offenders warning letters and after two or three of these the tenants' agreements were terminated. Those people would then find it difficult to find alternative apartments elsewhere in the city so were relegated to suburbs further outside or had to relocate to another town altogether.

I have no idea how they dealt with this problem these days where nearly half of the apartments are occupied by owner-occupiers. Another item of interest worth noting was that before the birth of intercom, young, pre-school children were sent up by the porter to find if the owner wanted to see a visitor. Naturally this additional service earned them extra pocket money.

The second drawback of this design is that during the summer heatwaves (which normally occurs between early June to late August) the courtyard could become a furnace without any air movement. The solution was to leave the large wooden front gate open and use the internal lockable iron gate. In the late afternoon they used to hose the central area in order to cool it. These days they use a sprinkler system.

Returning to our accommodation at 20, Maria Street which was a nunnery before the communist regime closed it down and evicted and dispersed the nuns.

I was allocated a room with two other chaps on the same course. The room was rather crowded with furniture, and we were hardly able to walk around as each of us had a bed, bedside locker, narrow gentleman's wardrobe, chair and largish desk where we did our work.

We partly solved this problem by turning the beds into bunks three stories high. I got the top one because of my parachuting experience and no fear of heights. The drawback was, in the high of summer, my bed was rather airless being so closed to the ceiling.

Each two or three dormitory rooms had a washroom with WC and cold showers. To compensate for the lack of hot water we were issued with a ticket each week for an indoor swimming pool. There, you could have a proper bath in the tub or could use the swimming pool. Nearly all of us chose to swim as we could have a hot shower there and have a good wash afterwards. I cannot think how we survived in the winter with no heating – we were obviously a lot tougher then).

Back at the nunnery we still had our caretaker who also had a further function to prevent ANY female from entering the building. We had a visitor's room next to the caretaker's office where we could be observed and could meet people regardless of the gender. We also had a large study on the ground floor where library type silence was imposed and allowed us to study in peace.

During the first year of our university course, we had to study in our curriculum, 13 subjects which included Marxism / Leninism, Russian language, higher mathematics, geometry, geography, research physics, theoretical mathematics and instrumentation etc.

Lectures were five hours in the morning and generally two in the afternoon, starting at 8am and completing at 2pm. Some afternoons were spent in tutorials.

The attendance was not compulsory, and nobody checked on us, as all university professors and lecturers had their own lecture notes covering the whole year on each subject which was duplicated and you could purchase these at an affordable price.

If you knew all that was written in them, you were brilliant. We could resell these lecture notes when we were done with them at virtually the same price for the next year pupils. The lectures went on six days a week but only in the morning on a Saturday. As you can see, we were extremely busy and with crammed lectures and studies. I cannot comprehend how Georgina only has so few subjects and a couple of days at university in comparison. I guess these days, with computers, you can do your own work easier.

I was doing quite well with all subjects but higher mathematics. As a budding scientist (or rather they tried to make us one) we were not allowed to accept any mathematical or physical formulae, but you had to arrive at those entirely by yourself using differentials and integration systems.

Although I wasn't too bad at maths, half of the time the lectures were well over my head, and I struggled with it.

I had a full scholarship and the money I received was enough to buy lecture notes or books (our accommodation was free) tram fares to and from university and purchasing canteen tickets for breakfast, lunch, and evening meals but I was only left enough to buy a few cigarettes which were dirt cheap at the time and to go out on Saturday for one glass of beer but no more.

To solve the problem, I skipped breakfast and evening meals. At lunchtime I would stay behind for about half an hour or so depending on the lecture schedule to clear the tables and stack them. For this service I was allowed to take away any bread or fruit that was leftover on the tables. On rare occasions I was offered leftover food, mostly on Saturdays.

I breakfasted on them and in the evening, I would use the bread and got some jam sent by my mother, sometimes with other foods which was carefully eked out till the next parcel delivery in about six weeks' time.

We used to visit the big, covered, central market on the Saturday afternoons where the stall holders would let us have fruit and veg which would have been thrown out on Monday.

I was permanently hungry although I didn't have any problem with being overweight, but I was seriously undernourished and needed a good feed up to improve my skeletal frame.

With all the money I'd saved from not paying for my food at the canteen I was able to have two or three small glasses of beer on Saturdays and an extra tram ticket to go out to the airfield once a week and to the cinema, possibly even stretching to taking a girl with me.

I was also able to buy with this cash a season ticket to the opera which were very heavily subsidised by the state for university students.

I carried on with my gliding career as it was entirely free. I joined MAV (Hungarian state railway) gliding club and we flew from an airfield at Farkashegy (Wolf Mountain) which is part of the Buda hills and kept on until I left the country in November 1956. During the more advanced gliding we used the uplift of the wind when it hit the side of the mountain.

There were extremely strict rules to adhere to when more than one glider was using the same mountain slope. The glider which had the right of way is the one with the slope on their right side and all other planes MUST give way.

On one occasion I was about 2000 feet high with the slope on my right (therefore I had right of way) and there were two other gliders on the same slope which were slightly below and above. The one below turned into my path (perhaps less experienced, careless or didn't see me) and struck my glider, braking off half of my left wing in the process. I was badly spinning but managed to get out of my glider. In a panic, I pulled my engage handle a little too early and the parachute was deployed. This slowed my fall but in my haste, I did not realise, as I'd never used a parachute before, that the broken wing was going to overtake me and then, when it happened it knocked me out. However, my parachute delivered my unconscious body to the ground safely without further damage.

I woke up in hospital all plastered up with a broken collar bone, one broken and one cracked rib and a broken upper arm. The other pilot managed to land his glider with only minor damage.

The other pilot's licence was suspended for six months and after that he was put on probation for a further year. If he had any further incidents, he would have lost his licence for good and never be allowed to fly solo again. This incident wrote off a glider, caused damage to another and put me in hospital with pretty serious injuries.

After that unpleasant experience I decided that it was time to learn about parachuting in case this ever happened again. I joined the Budapest parachute club, which was completely free, and, in the evenings, very intensive parachute training took place. I'm afraid my muscles were more used to sitting in a lecture theatre with occasional swim and athletics (100-meter sprint/ long jump) but after the parachute training session all my muscles were on fire, mainly at the bottom lower end of my body.

The training also included folding our own parachutes which was performed in a disused hanger with two folding tables. Each of those were about the size of six table tennis tables together. We were using standard army parachutes. We were paired up in two to fold the chutes under supervision of an army "jump master". When ready, we carefully marked our parachute and stacked them in rows for the next day jump.

The first jump was absolutely terrifying although none of us would admit it. We piled into an army Dakota which had all seats removed and substituted with a narrow bench on either side of the plane. About ten of us would sit on either side, totally terrified and secretly regretting our stupidity for volunteering in the first place. Before we flew over the drop zone we would stand in the centre, one tight behind the other. My main parachute would be tight on the chest of the chap behind, and the emergency parachute would be underneath the bottom of the person in front of me.

When the terrifying command came, we then hooked up our lifelines to a running rail at shoulder height. This would automatically open our chute about ten meters after we jumped out of the plane. The green light would come on accompanied with a command to jump. The last man in the line was the experienced one and would start to walk forward and we would have no choice but to shuffle forward until the door was reached and there was nowhere to go. The jump master, with a friendly but firm hand, would then shove us into nothingness.

The parachute opened and wrenched us upright and then I would feel completely elated, floating in total silence and enjoy the panorama which only lasted a few short minutes and soon the ground would start rushing towards our feet at incredible speed which allowed by gravitational laws. I swear it was a lot faster than that.

Our training clicked in and where we were busy stabilising our chute to stop it spinning and swinging you would grip the harness to soften your landing. With legs tight together we would then prepare for the parachute roll. We were elated after landing and could not stop telling everyone about our heroic experience whether they wanted to hear about it or not.

After the first jump it became less and less terrifying and actually became quite enjoyable. I mentioned earlier that it was compulsory to carry an emergency shoot. It was packed by a professional parachutist. I guess they didn't trust us completely. Just as well as much later we became more brazen and played tricks on each other, mainly to the two pretty girls in the club which we resented (male chauvinistic pigs) or perhaps because neither of them would go out with any of us. Sometimes we stayed behind after the folding sessions in the evenings and opening up their packed parachute we would carefully lift it out and give it a few twists before repacking them carefully. It would give a little fright as the parachute would only partially deploy and will trail above you as a very large fat sausage and give you a bit of a spin and fright but would eventually open out properly at (hopefully) a safe height. Later the girls would figure out our tricks, also figuring out the culprits and giving them the same treatment with a few extra twists to our parachutes.

Naturally we would "never" do this to a parachute which was used in free-fall as the 10-20 second delay to opening the chute would be very dangerous or even disastrous.

In these days we live in a society ruled by health and safety regulations. They would be horrified that there was absolutely no safety equipment. We jumped in our own city shoes, no helmets, no gloves as the harness webbing were likely to shave off the skin from our palms or hands. Also, a twisted unsupported ankle on an incorrect landing was common and frequent.

I have managed to achieve eight jumps in total, all of them from 800 to 1,000 metres (2,400ft – 3,000ft), that followed by two free falls and one night jump. The night jump was very exciting with only a torch attached by a six-foot string tied to your ankle which would give you about 1½ seconds warning before you hit the ground or perhaps, more accurately, the ground hit us. This jump was from 1,200 metres (3,600 feet).

The next jump planned was the water jump where you had to get out of your harness and let it go well before entering the water as you may get entangled in the canopy or webbing, or even result in drowning. We had a couple of boats on the lakes in case people got into difficulty. Unfortunately, I left the country before this planned water jump took place.

At the university, one of the compulsory subjects were Marxism and Leninism which were taken extremely seriously. This subject was to be taught in all universities whether you wanted to be a scientist, doctor, or economist. We had to study Karl Marx & Frederic Engels and Lenin's ideology on socialism and communism philosophy in all its detail. With six monthly exams to prove you really knew the subject.

By then I had lived under communism for about ten years and the original ideology and reality was vastly different. If the communism would have as been written by Marx and Engels, I would be the world's biggest communist.

I liked to call the communism a 'BUT', obviously not openly in society, as nearly everything has a 'BUT' attached to it. For example, one proudly proclaimed communist ideology is 'FREEDOM of RELIGION'. Yes, the churches would stay open, and you were free to go to the services, 'BUT' if you had been observed going to church you would be reported. Church going was frowned on by the communist ideology. You cannot be a good communist if you are a church goer so you would be reported to the party by a paid or unpaid snooper (there were thousands everywhere). As a result, you may be bypassed at your work for promotion, or your son or daughter may be denied a university place as a result for trying to exercise your right of 'Freedom of Religion'.

Another example of communist ideology was 'EACH CITIZEN HAS THE RIGHT TO FREE SPEECH', 'BUT', if you dared to criticise the government you were no longer considered to be a citizen as all citizens should support, whole heartedly, the government and its aims and plans.

I had a personal experience with this declaration. Whilst I was in university, I went to see a film with one of my room mates, Nicolas Varga. It was a dreadful dull and boring, rubbishy Russian, propaganda film. It was dubbed into Hungarian and when we were walking home, we both criticised this propaganda film very harshly. Suddenly, two burly policemen appeared and took us to the local police station and gave us a good beating. I had bruises all over my body, a black eye, and a bloody nose. Nicolas lost two of his teeth. After an hour and half, they let us go with a warning, this was only a 'friendly warning', next time they would give us a 'real beating'. We learnt our lesson that night about our actual 'Freedom of Speech'.

Another example was 'FREEDOM OF THE PRESS', 'BUT' you were only allowed to write anything if it did 'not' criticise the government or regime in any way. At the time you could not buy a newspaper, book, or magazine without seeing a line in the front pages which said 'Felelos Kiado' (English translation is 'Published By'). This was the responsible editor who was appointed by the party as a good, solid communist or pro-government whose job was to make sure that not a single word was printed of any anti-communist sentiment. This system even got into the realms of films, theatre, and opera, where every program declares the name of the "Felelos Kiado", the responsible producer.

I had a personal experience on the subject of the 'FREE ELECTIONS' ideology. Whilst at university an election was called and as there were no opposition in Hungary at the time. It was a one-party state. The question on the ballet paper was simply 'do you approve the government and their working?' If you agreed with the government, you would just fold your ballot paper in half and drop it in the box. 'BUT' there were no instructions what to do if you did not agree. Apparently, the results were published in some newspapers weeks after the ballot in some obscure section of the paper.

Also, some of the polling stations had their own special rules. Each polling station had two or three curtained booths, no desks to write on and no writing implements. Each station would have their own rules which was printed in some newspaper at some time before. One insisted on a cross for 'Yes' at one and a tick for 'No". Some had the opposite rule, some didn't require a mark at all and if you agreed then you would fold the paper without any marks and put it in the box. Some even insisted on a particular colour of ink, or the vote would be invalid and the paper destroyed.

Each university, office, factory, collective, country farm or even streets in towns had to march together waving the Hungarian flag to cast their votes. If you entered a booth to vote against the regime you were noted and reported as a suspected 'enemy of the state'. In this way, the system managed to publish over 95% participation and over 90%

agreement with their policies. This was in comparison to the 'rotten western capitalist state' having difficulties to produce even a 50% voting turnout in order to govern and go forward.

To sum up, the 'free and fair' communist election was a complete sham.

However, the state did look after their youth, providing free of charge facilities, education and included a very expensive glider and parachute training for 'the full enjoyment of the youth'. You may be waiting for a 'BUT' here so it's probably that these youths became fully trained sport parachutists. Using standard army equipment, they could be ready to don an army uniform and dropped behind enemy lines in case of conflict after a month or two of weapons training. The glider pilots, with only a few weeks of additional training, would have been able to fly large transport gliders towed to a target by a bomber or retrained for single seater powered aircraft to use in any impending war. They would have knowledge of basic flying, be physically fit, be regularly checked for this and be familiar with navigation equipment. They could also be used for surveillance or recognition or spotter missions. The generosity of the state for 'the enjoyment of the youth' was clouded by these ulterior motives.

One of the original Marxist theories is that in a true communist era you would not need money. Therefore, it would become a moneyless society where everybody works hard to their very best ability and the state will provide everything for your needs, home, food, clothing, and anything else.

All the shops and warehouses would stay open twenty-four hours a day, seven days a week where one would go in and help themselves to whatever they 'NEEDED'. In theory, you took one suit, overcoat, shoes, and tie and when this became unusable you would replace it for a new set. You would never dream to take two. Can you imagine a woman going into one of these stores for a new blouse and walk out with just a single blouse where there were all the colours and different styles? I do not think that this woman will ever be born.

Most of this ideology is a fantastic but unachievable Utopia. It would kill dead all human aspiration and achievements. What is the point to study and work hard if there is no reward for this?

Returning to my university course, I mentioned earlier that I was badly struggling with higher mathematics and, when I started my third year, there came an opportunity to change course. The university authorities had begun to realise that there would be too many mathematicians due to an unexpectedly low dropout rate, so there would be an oversupply situation and I was allowed to switch courses. In the communist regime there was to be no unemployment like in the 'rotten capitalist states.

On my new meteorology course there were four or five Albanian girls whose job, after qualifying, was to go home and start up their own meteorological office in Tirana, the capital of Albania.

At the beginning of our course, we made quite a few and not necessarily complimentary remarks to them as we stupidly thought that they would not understand. A few days later we heard them speaking perfect Hungarian. The joke was then on us.

Interestingly enough, our university was the only one in central and Eastern Europe and all the Balkans to offer meteorological courses. (I assumed that Moscow had one, but I do not know for sure).

I was offered a place in a technical university in Budapest to train as a structural engineer which I grabbed with both hands. In a basic core subject, I was over-qualified, but had to spend one month of my summer holiday to catch up with subjects which I had missed before I started the following September at my new university.

Once more returning to my synopsis of the communist ideology, I have to say that not all things were bad under the regime:

1) The State looked after the elderly and, actually, it was a truly free service. One did not have to pay a penny (Filler) towards our dentists, medication, hospital treatment or glasses and the system worked well. They looked after the elderly and disabled extremely well. I was rather surprised on one occasion when I stayed with Magdi, and Robbie and they got a visit from their GP. They explained that each doctor must visit at least once a fortnight to check the condition and medication of anyone over the age of 65.

2) The integrated transport system was centrally coordinated and good. For example, if a lorry had to deliver goods a long distance, they would always organise a load for the return journey.

3) All entertainment and sport were very highly subsidised by the State, culture being for all, not just the

rich.

4) Schooling, including universities, were entirely free and generally very good.

5) Public transport was reliable and cheap.

6) Wages were low, but the Government managed, year by year, eking the wages out and reducing the working hours. There were no deductions from your wages, what you earned is what you took home.

7) However, these items would not compensate my family for the confiscation of our land, farm, and the loss of income from them.

8) All the pensioners in the country could use buses, trams, underground and trolley buses in the cities totally free.

These days, these provisions for the elderly are still in place and also introduced free parking on Sundays in Budapest where normally it is virtually impossible, and it also entices people to come to shop and sightsee and enjoy themselves. The extra shopping also helped the local economy.

To add insult to injury, in about 1951 or 1952, our family house was confiscated while I was away at university. My stepmother was given one month to leave our home and she was 'billeted' in somebody else's house given one month to sell, giveaway or store our furniture as her new room would only take one single bed (a sofa bed when I was home on holiday). A largish wardrobe, chest of drawers and one armchair. She was also given part of a rather leaky barn to store her other furniture. However, the blistering, summer heat and damp, frosty winter did not do any good to the veneers of our French polished furniture.

She had to share the kitchen, bathroom, and toilet with the owner of her abode. It seems that this was the communist idea of solving the acute housing shortage instead of building new homes.

In Budapest, I tried to make some money by offloading bricks, cement, and other materials from railway wagons at night at some suburban railway or marshalling yard, sometimes at the weekends.

Saturday nights I spent four to five hours checking the TOTO (Hungarian football coupons). For a nights work we would receive about £1.00 - £1.50 worth of money. We also used to clear snow and ice on winter nights from the main roads and pavements earning roughly similar amounts of money.

The most interesting and satisfying way to earn extra money was tutoring. I did this in my second year at university. I was giving thorough revision to a boy called Atilla in mathematics and physics in preparation for his matriculation the next summer. The remuneration was to stay for a family evening meal for the day of my lessons which included a beer shared with Atilla's father. If I remember correctly, Atilla passed his subject with very high marks which I found this extremely satisfying.

Next year, recommended by Atilla's parents, I was tutoring twin girls, Maria and Katy in mathematics, algebra, and trigonometry. The remuneration was the same, a hearty meal with the family on the dates of the lessons. One of the twins matriculated to the top grade and the other was not as good but she managed a decent enough grade. The parents were so pleased that at the end of it the father gave me his Spanish stamp collection in which he was no longer interested but knew I was a stamp collector. After matriculation, Katie applied for a place at my university and was accepted but I cannot recollect which faculty she had ended up in.

Due to my 'starving years', starting with the winter of 1956 and during the siege of Budapest, where we were forced to eat dead horses as there was no other food at all. In the university, the food was extremely important to me and because of this upbringing, my dislike, even bordering on obsession, I hated, and still hate, to waste any edible food.

I must mention here that during my university years, Magdi and Frank were fantastic to me. They bought me a new suit every year to replace the, by then a very tatty, worn out one. After a whole year of constantly wearing, it at university where there was a strict dress code, so it became very worn out. You were always expected to wear a proper suit with shirt and tie. In the summer months, the tie could be removed, and you were also allowed shorts and sandals with socks. The suits were not that expensive but made with a very inferior cloth, even after six months it started to show its age and wear.

Magdi and Frank gave me two weeks summer holiday at Frank's parent's apartment in Gyor which was rather cramped with six of us. Franks parents were in one bedroom, and I was squeezed into a corner of Magdi and Frank's room and Uncle George (Frank's younger brother) had a sofa-bed in the dining room.

Mealtime was also rather crowded; breakfast was no problem with a slice of toast or something similar. I'd go out to eat at midday but the main meal in the evening was something easy and light made by Frank's mother as Magdi, Frank, George and Frank's father would still be working and normally eat at the work canteen. The bathroom would also get very busy, especially in the mornings.

Frank managed to get me a job for a week or so in his factory. I'd press heavy steel sheets in the workshop into certain shapes under supervision from the shop foreman. It was heavy work but in the very hot summer months we had to start at 6am and finish at 13:30 with an hour's lunch break. By 2pm, I was already in the swimming pool for the whole afternoon.

Life in Uniform

In Hungary there was compulsory national service in the 1950s of 27 months duration. Later this was reduced to 12 months by the late 1980s, and eventually abolished in 1990 completely, when professional soldiering started.

Every boy who reached the age of 18 was called up for this 27-month national service unless he was not physically fit. However, the university students were treated a bit differently as it was undesirable to suspend and interrupt their studies. So, each university, depending what subject you studied there, got affiliated to an army unit. For example, a student studying physics was allocated to a gunnery unit as basic knowledge in ballistics could be useful. Students studying civil engineering were connected to ordnance units of the Sappers.

We at the meteorological faculty were attached to an

anti-aircraft gunnery unit. We all had to study and take exams on all theoretical sides of the anti-aircraft work from tracery to the army ranks and aircraft recognition (western). In our classrooms we learnt the parts of all hand weapons taking them apart, cleaning and putting back together. This included rifles, submachine guns, and pistols. We were also instructed in the use of hand grenades, gas mask procedure and personal land mines.

It has just occurred to me that I don't know what happened to our female colleagues in the university as the Hungarian army had no female soldiers or even nurses. Did the girls take any exams in army subject or were they exempted and given knitting lessons instead, I wonder?

Every summer, we had to don an army uniform for one month and go through an army training camp which was usually located in the middle of very large field, miles, and miles from anywhere. I recollect that our nearest, tiny village was some three and half miles away from our camp and it didn't matter as in the first year we were not allowed to leave the camp anyway.

The second-year camp was in a large clearing in the middle of dozens of acres of conifer plantations. We were allowed out of camp for about four or five hours after the midday meal and evening roll call. On Sundays we hardly used this privilege as the village was several miles away and we were usually too knackered to go. Instead, we used the afternoon to write letters or relax for the first time in a week.

The camp usually housed about one hundred to two hundred of us, trained by a professional army sergeant in charge and corporals. Most of those were regular soldiers but some were also doing their national service which they were just about finishing. We all came under an officer, usually a sub-lieutenant or captain, who would visit us regularly and sometimes came unannounced to check our training and progress. Each of these officers had several camps under their control.

The regular servicemen resented us as spoilt, softy, townies, getting away with just a few months instead of the normal two years plus, to pass in soldiering service. The day of arriving at the camp, we were given brand new army boots that had never been broken in and we had to undertake a ten-mile route march on our second day with full equipment which coincided with the hottest time of the day. The march consisted of a 50-minute march with a ten-minute break. The Kapca was a piece of triangular linen cloth folded skillfully around our feet to act as a sock (we were not allowed to use our own socks). Due to our inexperience of folding this piece around our feet, the cloth wad just became a lump somewhere in our boots and we were given lots more blood blisters from the new boots.

When arriving to the camp all our personal items were put into canvas holders with the exception of a comb, toothbrush, toothpaste, and shaving gear. Our uniform was standard army, one dubiously colored pair of underpants, one vest, trousers, tunic, wide leather belt, small towel and three or four Kapca. All these were changed each Saturday for clean ones. Sometimes if there was very heavy rain, we had to scrape off the mud from our trousers and tunic as we had to wear it until the following Saturday. Of course, we were given a rifle which was expected to be kept in perfect condition and it was vigorously inspected each and every day and taken very seriously. There was no place in our tent to keep them clean and dry so we would usually take them to bed with us and joking that it was our wife lying next to us each night.

Our tent was where four of us were housed (it was much smaller than our present sun lounge in the UK). It was sunk into the ground, some three feet deep with the spoils carefully banked up on all sides except the narrow gap at the front which was the entrance which had two steps down. The tent was supported by a central post and stretched over so that the rain would stay outside. Sides were internally supported by locally harvested shrubs and branches to keep most of the earth falling into our beds which were on a slightly raised platform. We had straw filled mattresses and our bedding included two stiff army blankets. We usually laid one of these on the straw mattresses to make it less harsh on our backs. We had a bunk either side of the central space which were not enough for the four of us to stand up together and another two bunks at the end. The worst things were the pillows that were filled with lumpy sheep wool which was also extremely smelly. We often wondered if part of the sheep was still there as it smelled so bad.

We did not have any bed sheets or pillowcases and were given a small canvas bag to hold our toiletries and this was hung from the central pole.

All the erection of the tents, digging new latrines etc. were done by regular soldiers or national servicemen prior to us arriving to the camp.

Life in the camp was very hard and harsh. We had to

get up at 5am and after a quick wash and shave in cold water. At eighteen/nineteen years old our whiskers were not that prevalent, and we managed to get away with one single shave per week. By six o-clock, we were fully dressed, even in these conditions the blankets had to be folded perfectly flat otherwise the whole tent's occupiers were punished by a 'communal punishment'. The punishment was usually in the evening, depending on our crime it was usually to run around the encampment multiple times. Each circuit was about one mile and in extreme cases we would have to run it fully loaded with all our equipment.

The camp was self-sufficient with our own mobile cooking facilities, laundry, and hot water supply (occasionally) but they tapped into the local water main. There was no gas or electricity, so we had to get local wood by cutting down trees with axes and two handled cross saws and carry them back to the camp. This was done on a rotation basis to keep the fuel hungry boilers working and to keep the cooks happy.

All was helped by 'volunteers'…" You and you - REPORT TO THE COOKHOUSE!" Duties were usually peeling endless buckets of potatoes and veg using our own penknives. The bread must have been baked on site as I cannot remember any bread deliveries happening.

By 6.15am we were queuing for our breakfast which was a pint or so of sweet, black coffee, laced with bromine which was regulation and a large piece of bread and tiny piece of jam no bigger than a walnut.

When I asked the local pharmacist for information on the bromine, she told me that this drug is a sedative to make people calm and relaxed. In Hungary during the 1950s homosexuality was against the law and taken very seriously. If anybody was caught in the act you would be jailed for up to five years on the first occasion and considerably more for subsequent occasions. The army used bromine to suppress any sexual desires.

The pharmacist lady told me "You were all drugged in the army all of the time". Actually, it was true, but never thought or realised it at the time. Interestingly, in my own experience, if you were inclined that way, you were generally to knackered to even think about it as all you really wanted to do was lie down and go to sleep.

We would eat our breakfast (and bromine) fast as we had to be on parade at 6.30am, lined up for inspection including our rifles. To keep our boots shining was an impossible task. The distance between the tent and the parade ground was dusty or muddy, so we would walk to the parade bare foot and then put them on when we got there as we could never make it without getting them dirty. Thank goodness they did not inspect our muddy or very dirty feet.

At 6.45am we marched out in a beautifully lined column to our training ground, whether it was square bashing, a route march or digging firing pits for anti-aircraft guns which had to be sunk 18 inches below ground level to stop them rolling when being fired. We actually never fired a live shell except dummies until the end of our second-year camp when we actually fire live ammunition at a foolhardy pilot in a small aircraft towing a very long rope a target sock.

At 1pm we would be marching back to our camp for

our lunch which usually consisted of bowl of soup, and we started queuing for the second course whilst eating this, standing up. We were eating 'on the hoof'. The second course usually was some kind of stew with brown bread, and we would eat this in the queue waiting for the final course. A pint of sweet, black coffee, apple or pear or a handful of grapes if in season.

At 1.30pm we would be marching out again for our afternoon session and back at 7pm for our evening meal which often was a helping of left-over stew from lunchtime, but sometimes some pasta dish would come our way with a pint of sweet black coffee, laced with bromine.

This routine went through the week apart from Sunday, which was free, in theory. We actually sat down at trestle tables for the first time in seven days where we could actually eat and relax.

To my very big surprise, I excelled myself on the firing range, with nearly top score in rifle and pistol shooting but I let myself down with the score with the sub-machine gun which I found had a mind of its own.

At the end of the month of purgatory, I was marked down as "officer material" and was promoted to corporal with my first stripe on my shoulder.

The campsite was used two or three times in a season and, when we finished, the national servicemen stayed back to take down the camp and everything in it. All our personal clothes were returned in exchange for our uniform which had been carefully laundered in a mobile laundry also in rotation with our blankets and pillows.

The national servicemen emptied all our straw

mattresses and made a huge bonfire with it.

Our hatred for our sergeants and corporals by l this time had evaporated when we got back into civilian clothes, and they no longer seemed so scary.

The army officers were harsh, but they still managed to make soldiers out of a bunch of softies.

What did surprise me was the comradeship we built up whilst in the army. One of the lowest points was our route march and blood blisters to go with it than you could count. We helped the stragglers as much as we could by carrying their backpacks and equipment in spite of our own suffering and needs but some of us were, borrowing Joe's favourite expression, a "smidgen" fitter than the others. We had a motto that translated as "don't let the buggers beat us", referring to the sergeants and corporals and this worked well to help us along.

The second-year camp was not as bad as the first. Perhaps we toughened up a bit by then and learned some of the dodges of the army, like 'NEVER' volunteer for anything in spite of possible rewards and 'NEVER' let the instructors see you sitting down otherwise you would be 'volunteered' for various duties. My single stripe helped me to avoid some of the more tedious work.

The second-year camp was located in a large clearing of a vast conifer forest which had the advantage of avoiding the stifling heat, but we paid for this little comfort as we had to endure the endless armies of mosquitos, mainly during the night. Sleeping was virtually impossible with no sheets to cover us, and we could only use the clean Kapca or our grubby damp towels. There was a contest of oppressive heat versus mosquitos. That year, we were the first intake in the camp, so we had laundered blankets and much less smelly pillows. It had also another advantage of the forest and firewood was easy to locate and provide for our cooks.

One week our platoon was detailed to guard duties. One man to guard the clothing warehouse, two for the armoury, two at the ammunition dump and one for the flag at the parade ground.

We had four hours on and four off with the exception to the guard of the flag as he had to stand virtually motionless was changed every two hours. The other advantage of that detail was that they had the whole night off as the flag was only up from sunrise to sunset.

As I believe I mentioned before, our extremely vigorous training pushed all of us to virtual exhaustion. We could sleep anywhere including standing up or on bare concrete floors.

My single stripe gave me a distinct advantage. I was able to choose my guard position which I thought was the best. I chose guarding the clothing warehouse. During the day there were no problems but at night it was very difficult to keep awake as our sergeant and corporals had a tendency to creep up on us to check our alertness.

One night I was slumped against the main entrance to the warehouse. I dozed off and suddenly woke up, not by a noise but by a feeling that something was not right. Opening my eyes, I saw a very large rat sitting on his hind legs on my chest, less than six inches from my nose and with his beady black eyes he kept looking at me. I could swear that he or she was winking at me, fancied me or thought I was a bit skinny, but I could still feed not only his family but the whole tribe of rats for weeks. I am not sure which one of us had the bigger fright discovering each other's presence when I eventually moved. As my rat was sitting on my chest outside the warehouse there must have been many, many more inside which could not have been good for all the clothing stored there.

For the guard duties all of us got two rounds of ammunition, both blanks, with the exception of the guards at the armoury and ammunition dump. They received one blank and one live. At the end of the second army stint, I was doing quite well and was given my second stripe and promoted to a sergeant.

The system was that after the third summer stint you would become a Sergeant Major (if doing well) and when you completed your university degree you would be called up for six months in an army training camp. On passing you would then be prompted to 'Alhadnagy' which was the lowest officer rank in the regular army.

I returned to the University in the autumn to the course which I really enjoyed but some two or three months later I went to collect my monthly scholarship money when they said there was nothing for me. I queried the absence of the cash, and this was, in a way, a rebellious and an offensive gesture where in a communist state you were just supposed to accept the officials or superiors' decision without question. Eventually a rather masculine looking, bad-tempered female came out to see me after an hour long wait and told me that somebody overheard me criticising the regime or party. She told me that "you cannot expect the State to pay for your education as you obviously dislike, resent or hate the system". It was noted that this was not my first brush with the authorities. She actually referred to the incident a year or so before when the police beat us up for criticising the Russian cinema film. I had, therefore, lost my scholarship at that point.

She also told me I was lucky not to be kicked off the University, but the State would no longer pay and as my stepmother would or could not help me. I reluctantly had to leave and find a job and accommodation as I could no longer continue my studies.

There were quite a few prominent and rather vocal individuals in the country but due to their position could not easily be silenced who constantly and severely criticised the shortcoming of the regime.

One of these people I knew of was Cardinal Joseph Mindszenty, the primate of all Catholics in the country. In every sermon given during Sunday mass, he would severely condemn and criticise the Communist regime from the safety of his pulpit. He had been warned numerous times and he also had to submit the contents of his forthcoming sermons but when he stood up in the pulpit, he would tear the scrypt into pieces and scatter them over the people and continue to criticise and condemn the communists. He had a 'show trial' to demonstrate how fair the regime was and was sentenced to several years in prison. Even then, he could not be stopped, and he was put in solitary confinement. When his sentence had been served it all began again and there was yet another 'show trial' and another sentence to follow. All in all, he spent the best part of ten years in the nick until in 1956 when the revolution let him out but by then he had become a broken old and very ill man.

When the Russians crushed the resistance and started to dish out the heavy-handed punishments to anyone who dared to oppose them, Mindszenty asked for, and was given, asylum in the American embassy.

A few years later a petition was made in Hungary with thousands of signatures to the Vatican asking to elevate him to sainthood for all his sufferings. However, the petition was turned down by Rome as his sufferings were political and not religious reasons. I lost sight of him and had no idea where or when he died.

Interestingly, when Anne and I were in Australia in 2004, we found a bust of the Cardinal in the Catholic cathedral in Sydney which was labeled 'commissioned by and paid by the Hungarian expats.

The other unstoppable critic was a professor, but I cannot recollect his name, but he was the head of the mathematics faculty of the technical university in Budapest. He was internationally well known, publishing several books and papers on various mathematical theorems and incidentally, professor doctor Erno Rubik, the inventor of the Rubik cube, was working under him. I actually attended one of his legendary lectures but, disappointingly, he kept strictly to mathematics.

Before I leave my favourite subject of Communist-bashing, I should recall a conversation with Zsuzsa. As a qualified meteorologist, she was employed at the 'Ferihegy', which is the biggest international airport in Hungary, to brief the pilots on weather conditions that they expected on their routes. There were normally a team of five. Generally, when they arrived on their shifts, for about 20 minutes or so they discussed TV, theatre, cinema and love life or other problems. They then got down to work for a few hours, then a coffee break with a lot more chatting, more work, dinner, and more chat. In her own admission, the work for the five could have been done comfortably done by four, or even three.

This is how the State solved the problem as 'only the rotten Western capitalism have unemployment' – here, they were creating over-employment to control the problem. I just realised that it was a surprise that the authorities allowed me to change my university course when they realised the oversupply of meteorologist and lack of structural engineers.

At the airport, Zsuza (Suzanna) met Imre Szerenyi, who also worked there. They fell in love and later got married. After some years, Suzana got pregnant but lost the baby and that seemed to be the cause of their marriage breakup.

Before leaving Budapest, one final interesting event took place. In about 1953-4, Hungary experienced an unusual cold spell of cold winter weather. The temp dropped below -15C and the Danube was partly frozen up. By the fluctuation of the river level, it caused in some places, the ice to break up and large sheets of this, some of them six-nine inches thick, managed to slide on top of each other and froze together. This then formed a mini iceberg. The fast-flowing Danube then carried these down the river and the western branch of the river round Margaret Island was frozen, forcing the flow on the other side to speed up dramatically. The river was hurling these icebergs down, threatening the supporting legs of the bridges with damage or even possible destruction.

The Government sent in dive bombers to bomb and break up these obstructions. Perhaps there was 'a slight' exaggeration as Hungary only had one dive bomber on lease from the Russians at that time.

They were nothing like the famous Stukas which, with a terrifying high-pitched screech, were designed to disorientate and intimidate the enemy. They bombed the area by the Margaret Bridge after closing both bridges and riverbanks. They started their bombing runs and we went halfway up Gellert Mountain to see the spectacle. Unfortunately, by then, when we reached our view point the bombing was nearly over and we only caught the last three bombs hitting the icebergs with extremely huge amounts of water, ice, and steam.

These days Lali informed me that the Government purchased the most advanced ice breaker ships recently which would break up the ice before it could become too dangerous. The ice breaking ship is so successful at clearing ice that it now clears not only the entire Danube but the Tisza as well each winter. Lali also informed me that the Government purchased a second ice breaker to clear in the Danube in the Romanian, Bulgarian and Serbian sections as they too had no ice breakers, and this is a very lucrative contract for the country earning considerable amounts of well needed foreign currency. He also informed me that this winter (2017) also produced very low temperatures and the breakers were working 24 hours a day to keep the waters navigable.

Chapter 6 - Joining The Wage-Slaves

There was a fantastic system in Hungary in the mid-to-late 1950s, which worked beautifully if you wanted new employment. If, for any reason whatsoever you left your present job, the ex-employer had to notify the central employment office and your name, details, previous employment record, qualification and experience were recorded, and they would then try to match these with any available vacancies.

In my case, the University notified the employment office that I was no longer a student there and was therefore looking for work. As I had no previous work experience, they matched me with the subjects I was studying which included Geology, Geodesics, Statistics and Climatology. The matching was done manually at first, then later, a punch card system was introduced which speeded up the process. Later, computers took over.

I was matched within a week, and this was based on my short studies in statistics, to a branch office of the national statistical service. There were some twenty staff working in this dingy basement office in one of the Budapest suburbs.

In my section there were eight of us, including myself, three boys and five girls. We were given pages and pages, reams, and reams of data to put in order, tabulate it and most of the time evaluate and produce graphs of the results which provided bar or pie charts.

We had no idea what the data related to, it could have been about production figures of a coal mine, average water volume flowing down the Danube River through Budapest, government tax receipts or relations between divorce rates and marriages.

All in all, it was a completely mind-scrambling and soul-destroying experience. Interestingly enough, I had to say that in the long term, it would send me to drink but as I couldn't afford that I'd probably just have to commit suicide instead! My colleagues did not seem to mind it, even enjoyed it, and one student studying university statistics absolutely loved it. Interesting to see how it shows how the male and female brains were wired up.

During these tortuous months, I was lucky to find a room to rent, as at the time the housing shortage was quite acute in Budapest. It was a basement flat and very dingy. Just enough room for a bed, a bedside cabinet, chair, and tiny wardrobe with zero cooking facilities. I couldn't even make up a cup of tea. The bathroom facilities were shared between the family of the owner of the flat, me and a second lodger. Hot water was available for one hour each morning and one in the evening.

You could have one bath on Saturday evening, but if you missed your slot for any reason you would have to go dirty for another week. The food was also a problem, so I lived on Kolbasz (Hungarian Sausage), bread, cheese, paprika, tomatoes, apples and any other seasonal fruit and would eat them all in my tiny basement pad. Once a week, I was just able to afford a proper, cooked meal in a nearby side street bistro.

I was lucky that after some two and half months of purgatory, it came to an end as I received an offer for some ordnance survey work with the National Geodesic and Cartography firm of the BGTV, a branch office at Pecs which I grabbed with both hands.

I gave two weeks' notice for my lodging and moved to Komlo. From here, the first batch of my new work was to be conducted. The employment system rules meant that when you got a job offer you were not allowed to reject it but if you were unhappy after six months you could start looking again. If you were to refuse and leave early, then they would not look again at getting you employment again until those six months were up. If you had no savings or money, the state would not help you in the meantime, so you just starved.

If you were unhappy with the salary or wages, you had no choice at all and you were pigeonholed by your qualifications and experience, and you would stay there until you gained extra qualifications or seniority. Not unlike our civil servants. Your job was set to your grading and there was nothing you could do about it.

In my case, I got a set salary, but with quite a few extras for the field work and the work away from your base, plus bonuses if you exceeded your target which, together would effectively double up your salary. I was saving very seriously, to be able to buy a small motorbike, Csepel, a 200cc engine to use it to go to and from work to give some relief to my two, poor, worn out and faithful ponies (according to the Hungarian folklore, everyone had two ponies, the right and the left foot – i.e., Peter and Paul so there was no excuse not to use them). I saved nearly enough money to purchase this bike by the end of 1956.

In the mid-1950s in Hungary, everything was working on a strict cash only basis. Hire purchase did not exist and to borrow any cash was impossible unless you did this privately, or from friends and family for larger purchases.

They had no idea about sales or discounts, offers etc. in Hungary. These words didn't even come into the vocabulary until the mid-1950s.

Komlo is a small mining town in the Mecsek hills, mining a very inferior, brown coal which straight away fed into the electricity generating plant built next door to the mine head.

We were installed in a brand new, two-storey hotel, which had some thirty or thirty-five bedrooms, half facing the main town square and the other half faced the town's swimming pool.

We could actually go through the ground floor rear entrance, directly into the pool area as this facility was included in our bill when you stayed in the hotel. I got a very nice second floor room, looking out to the square which was quite roomy and light and with a biggish desk, which I had to work at during the evening on the data that was collected whilst performing the field work.

The main square of the town had a statue in the middle and a beautifully maintained garden with lots of flowerbeds. The hotel was a commercial hotel used only by visiting officials and staff connected to the mine or power plant. No tourist would go there on purpose at all.

Apart from the hotel there were a few dozen houses, a tiny primary school, small town hall, general store/bistro with e-a tiny restaurant which we used when we were not working out in the field. Whilst away, we would live on some bread, cheese, sausage fruit and a large bottle of water for our lunch which we had to carry at all times in our backpack.

The hotel had no restaurant, and at the time in Hungary, B&B's did not exist.

One of our first tasks was that in our team or 4-5 surveyors was to measure the Komlo area as the authorities wanted to extend the mine by opening a new pit head plant after discovering extra-large seams of coal.

After we finished this task, we were levelling between and triangulation points. We used roads and each of us got our stretch which we had to co-ordinate between us weekly so if there were any mistakes in the measurements and calculations the result would be disastrous, and we would have to go back and re-measure everything for no extra money.

The measurements had to be extremely accurate as we were only allowed less than a half inch grace in a distance of one kilometre. We had to carry all our kit, the theodolite with telescopic, folding legs and the staff would carry the other measuring instruments. We had three helpers with us, two in charge of the staff who would set these up with a distance of about a hundred metres from each other and there would be me in the middle, working with a clerk (usually a schoolboy or girl who had to write very fast and accurately the back and front readings I would give from the theodolite and also record the distances). One digit out and the day's work would be wasted, and we would have to repeat the whole process.

The man at the back site quickly had to move forward, leapfrogging us, and become the front site.

The surveyor had to set up his theodolite, and level it accurately with two sets of levelling bubbles in the instrument. In about twenty to thirty seconds, he would be ready for the first reading. If one spent more time than that, we would not be able to achieve the target for the day's measurements (ten kilometres per day of measurements). If we failed, this would reduce our wages.

We had to telephone the local labour office every evening to book our labour requirements for the next day. We started from the hotel at six o'clock or six thirty at the latest as we may have to walk up to half an hour before we reached the starting point for the day. If this was more than four kilometres, it triggered a larger mileage allowance considering that after our hot and sweaty day's work we would have to lug all our kit back to the hotel using our 'two ponies'.

Saturdays were normal working days in Hungary, and we tried to work to tabulate and calculate our data from the week.

We used a very complex, but excellent calculating machine called "Brunswiga." It was, at the time, in the absence of any electronic calculator, the only tool able to deal with nine- or ten-digit figures to make the calculations required.

The calculator was working entirely by a set of very clever arrangements of cog wheels and needed to be wound by a handle quite furiously to and fro, the same time moving the cursor. The required figures would arrive eventually with the correct figures, but progress was slow.

It was exactly like the Enigma machine from the Second World War that broke the Germans code, and both worked on the same principle. Not surprisingly, both machines were developed and made in West Germany.

Our normal work routine was that in that very hot summer, we would make a very early start and then we would manage to get home late PM, and after carefully storing our instruments and equipment in a secure storeroom provided by the hotel, we could remove our dusty, sweaty clothing and dash down to the swimming pool having a compulsory shower beforehand and then diving into the lovely cool water. The pool was Olympic-sized.

I had noticed before, a rather pretty, dark haired, well-formed, and tanned girl of about 18yrs old in a tiny and revealing bikini. (I do not know, as the song said, if it was the "incy-winsy-teeny-weeny, yellow polka dot bikini" or not, but I was bowled over by the girl). One evening after I'd finished my swimming, I'd got out to return to my room through the back door of the hotel. The pool was allowed to be used by the hotel management as it was included in the room rates. One evening, suddenly, two girls followed me from behind and threw me into the pool amid lots of laughing about my predicament. The swimming pool had a kerb so they had to push me with some great force to get me in there.

The following day, I waited until my pool assassins were finished swimming and had got dressed to go home. I picked one of them up and threw her in. As her head came back out of the water, I was expecting torrents of complaints and cursing but instead of that, I got full hearted laughter and giggles… just one complaint, "look at the state of my hair, what does it look like, I just shampooed it!". After my ungentlemanly act, I then offered my hand to pull her out of the pool but something in her cheeky eyes warned me, so I was ready for her when she then tried to pull me in, as I had predicted.

After that rather unorthodox and wet introduction, according to the dreadful American expression, we became 'an item'. Inseparable. There is a saying that when in love, there must be chemistry between the two. In our case, chemistry was in overdrive. We would go on a daily swim together, went walking over evening and weekends in the surrounding woods which at the time was full of wild strawberries which were juicy and sweet. You couldn't walk a step without squashing a dozen of them. We ate ourselves silly and collected punnets of them for her to take home.

In the evening we went down to the only local bistro for a glass of wine and beer. Her name was Marika (Maria) and she eventually took me to her home and introduced me to her parents, which terrified me but it turned out much better than expected.

I got on well with her father as he was also a surveyor, but dealt predominantly with mines, and our work was similar but mine was above and his was below the ground. His work was definitely much more difficult in the labyrinth of shafts and tunnels and five to six different levels including all the mine explosions of methane gas. There was also a danger of flooding down there all which I did not have to deal with.

I got on well with her mother as well as she was passionate about operas, and we did have long discussions on the subject. Marika was their only child and the apple of their eyes, and a rather clever girl. On her matriculation, she did very well compared to my mediocre achievements.

During that summer, I was all alone for a few days and more than one person asked me if we had had 'a lover's tiff'. She actually had to travel to Szeged, a very large town or city in the south of the country near the Yugoslavian border for the entry interview exams as she wanted to become a doctor. The University offered her a place with a full scholarship.

Our relationship had the understanding that at some stage we would get married, however, her family was very keen to formalise this arrangement before she went to university and decided to have a large engagement party at Szilvester (Saint Sylvester's eve, 31st December i.e. New Year's Eve). They had quite a large extended family, lots of Aunties and Uncles, all of whom I never met.

It would have been interesting to note that the electricity generating plants turbines was responsible for heating the swimming pool we first met in, and instead of pumping, the excess heat generated by the turbines to heat the hotel and other buildings including the cottages used by the miners and the plant employers.

The pool was always warm even if outside it was minus 10 degrees in the winter, so still usable.

The next job was more interesting; it was a project as the work of remapping the borderline between Hungary and Austria after the tension between eastern and western blocks had decreased and the Sappers had removed and blown-up mines and removed the electrified border fences.

This border was actually part of the famous, or rather infamous iron curtain between eastern and western Europe. We went in to check and re-map all the border posts (concrete blocks, dug into the ground) some were damaged or dislodged by bulldozers clearing the ground to start farming again.

During our work, each of us were given one or two labourers to clear the overgrowth, mainly of stinging nettles as high as six-foot, dense brambles or other creeping plants.

It was very interesting to see how quickly nature reclaimed its territory. It was miles and miles of vacant strip of land which was only interrupted by the crossing of a few roads, railway lines and very infrequent small rivers.

These days, the buzz word is to help wildlife and nature. In this case the strip of vacant land, made up with a fifty-metre-wide strip with a wire fence with frequent warnings beyond this was a mine field, then an actual ten-foot-high border fence, a narrow strip used by the border guards for foot patrol which sometimes included dogs. The 'no-man's land' on the Austrian side had a similar arrangement giving the total of some 300–400-foot strips of land.

Four teams were working in there, given a length of two kilometres of the strip with which to complete. When we completed our allocated our patch, one would leapfrog over the other.

I was allocated to start working northwards, starting at the 'triple point': the boundaries between Hungary, Yugoslavia, and Austria. The point which I found most favourable for a perspective escape route later, perhaps because the southern borders of Yugoslavia were less heavily defended. I understand this was not mined, as Yugoslavia was a communist country with their leader, Marshall Tito, who was a very clever politician, who managed to steer the country into their own version of Communism, and they made their own rules and were not imposed on by the hard line authorities in Moscow. Keeping friendly with the Russians, but at the same time staying friendly with the West and doing business with both. Often, they would play one side against the other. This boosted their economy well. It is perhaps a good parallel with this situation and the current problem with Brussels as we are experiencing today with Brexit.

In my strip, we found a lot of evidence of casualties of the mines by animals, finding skulls of badgers, deer, wild boar, foxes. Only the skulls remained as all other parts of the animals had been eaten by other animals. Finally, anything left was cleaned up beautifully by the ants.

One of my colleagues started a skull collection, the largest was a wild boar's skull which sat proudly on the top of his wardrobe in his bedroom and the smaller ones took up the rest of his room, even sacrificing part of his bathroom shelf to display his collection.

I cannot recollect exactly which of the trophies were found by me, but I think it was a three-year-old deer as his antlers had three prongs and became the second-best exhibit hanging on the free-standing hotel coat hanger.

One of the other team members also working on the southern end found a human skull, uncomfortably close to my starting point. This was surprising as the border guards very carefully removed all traces of any human casualties. We obviously notified the authorities, who would send out a forensic team and collect all the other bones and also come to the conclusion that he was not blown up by a mine but got entangled in some disused barbed wire and brambles as he tried to use this riverbed as an escape route but was drowned in the swollen river during the wet season.

On one very hot day we decided to have our midday lunch break by a rotten old tree trunk which we used conveniently to lean against. We would settle down and eat our sandwiches except our labourers, a large and fat man who would not settle down and would turn this way and that, eventually got on his knees to try and clear the leaves and twigs and other vegetation in his chosen position. Suddenly, with a big scream, he jumped up at the speed a young athlete would be proud of. His white face was pointed at his previous position, and we could see a bright detonating plate, now exposed where he had sat.

Naturally we suspended any further work until the mine was dealt with and notified the police on our return to the hotel who then informed the bomb disposal squad.

Next day, I received a telegram which said that "the mine has been neutralised which was missed by the mine clearing team, perhaps because of its close proximity to the stump".

Rather cruelly, we teased our big fat friend thereafter that only his big fat arse managed to save his life because his load was spread out over a larger area and didn't set off the mine.

Returning to the site the following morning, we found a large hole in the ground and our tree was lying on the side some three foot away. Obviously, the bomb disposal team decided to blow the whole thing up rather than endangering themselves trying to diffuse it.

Thinking about all the skeletons we found, we wondered how they managed to get blown up in the first place. We understood that the weight of a wild boar or large stag would have easily triggered the mine switches but couldn't figure out how the weight of something like a fox would have caused it to blow up. We guessed that a badger digging round the mine might have cause it but not a fox.

The answer came from my cousin Lali, who was a qualified civil engineer and his work sometimes involved explosives during his national service. He learnt how to lay and diffuse mines during this time. In his opinion, some mines were linked together, three, four, even five. Generally, escapees would never try to cross the border on their own, so the mines were wired together to take out groups. Therefore, if one large animal triggered the mine, several others would go off for maximum damage and obviously, other animals were caught in the collateral killing.

As we continued our work of remapping the border line, we were given maps of the very latest version of the location of each mine as we would need them to stay safe.

At the hotel one night, we looked at those maps and could not see any pattern to when they were originally laid. When one of our colleagues joined us and became astonished about our ignorance. He told us that there was a clever system, the knight (from a chest set) could move three x one way and x one in another 90 degrees on a board and the mines were laid in the same way. Naturally, the person who designed this layout was a chess player.

This was about the time when Hungarian football was at its best, Puskas Kocsis (the big Hungarian national team) got up to the semi-finals of the world cup and only West German managed to beat them. We sat by the radio listening to this (no TV at the time) and were jumping and screaming for Hungary to win and the horrible Germans to lose.

Hungary played against England at the time and managed to beat them at Wembley (3-6) on the 25th of November 1953, which was a very big deal because nobody had ever beaten the English team before at home. The return match was in the "Nepstadium" (people's stadium) which has now been renamed at "Puskas Ferene stadium". On the 25th of May, there was a return match with England in 1954 and Hungary won again with a score of 7-1.

I was in the parachute competition – I cannot recollect the details, but the top 3 competitors were given the honour of jumping out of a small plane to parachute down over the stadium before the kick off.

One person would be carrying the match ball and the other two would be carrying two large bouquets of flowers for the football captains. As it happened, one of the parachutists was a girl who was very suspicious, as in the club there were only four girls and forty boys but miracles will happen. Was this a political stunt or manoeuvre we wondered?

We were at the airport, extremely excited and hyped up, and were about to start taxiing out in the jump plane when a red flare suddenly shot across our bows which was the sign for "abort".

The Met Office stopped us because the wind speed had increased, and it had become too dangerous for a jump over a built up area where hitting the target was paramount and you could only allow for a few feet margin of error. After that, we then all piled in the airport commander's jeep and drove at breakneck speed to the stadium to see only the last ten minutes of the game.

Now, to return to my story at the southwest corner of the country where we were re-measuring the exact border line with Austria. We were completely cut off from all civilisation and news in this remote corner of Hungary. Populated by small farms and homesteads. These people would go to the nearest village on market days once a week, fortnight, or month where they would take their surplus goods and animals to sell and exchange for items they needed until the next market day.

There were no telephone lines and no electricity in these tiny hamlets, we stayed in these during the week to save hours of walking from the base and the local farmers were glad for the additional income to let their spare bedrooms out on a B&B basis which often included sharing their evening meals for little extra cash.

The Government's five-year plan pledged that all villages and hamlets of more than ten houses would get connected to the electricity grid so radios could then be used as at the time, battery radios were not available in Hungary even though they were invented in the 30s.

The first time we heard of the 'October Hungarian revolution' from the crew which were working to electrify these hamlets and villages which was a great surprise to us. There were small bits of evidence that the extremely hard line, unbending regime started to bend just that little bit.

The Iroszovetseg (writers club) were allowed to publish weekly literature which quite often criticised the communist regime and it seems that opposition in the country was starting to finally pick up speed and find its nerve and voice.

Fighting the Russians in the 1956 Uprising (Initial Thoughts)

The uprising was initially established as a protest by Hungarian students. The intention was to remove the Russians from their country so they could select their own government. The ARVO (the Hungarian Secret Police) turned machine gun fire on students, killing a dozen of them. This was the key flashpoint. Incensed, the students took over the broadcasting station, disarming a policeman who was guarding it. At that time, I was living next to the radio station.

Students used the radio station to broadcast, encouraging the uprising for a few days. In contrast, there was another radio station called Free Europe. In fact, it was an American propaganda machine reporting that 10,000 troops were waiting to liberate the people of Hungary. These reports helped to prolong the fighting, killing many, many more people. What was fascinating about the uprising was that it was entirely spontaneous, fuelled by anger. It was very much a collective approach.

The students had captured an intact Russian tank, placing a Hungarian flag on top. The Russians blew it to pieces. They weren't alone in guerrilla fighting, children also played their part in destroying tanks. Both students and children took out other tanks, ambushing them in narrow roads where the gun turrets couldn't pivot around. They approached them from behind with hand grenades. The children planted land mines as well so that the troops had to physically get out and remove them. When they did the guerrilla fighters shot them.

We reached a point where we realised that we couldn't beat the Russians. Tens of thousands of young Hungarians then tried to get out of the country when this happened.

There was one occasion where I was involved with the uprising. I was at university, watching a Russian propaganda film with a friend. Spies were everywhere in the University; in every office, in every class, reporting any criticism to the Russian society whatsoever. My friend and I took the tram home. We were quite clear about the film and what we really thought if it. When we got off the tram, we noticed two men following us who then took us to the police station where we were beaten.

I was lucky, my bruises were pretty light. My friend lost four teeth and had his kidneys damaged. We were both released but were told this was a warning, the next time would be much worse if we got caught again.

I wouldn't class myself as a guerrilla fighter, just one of 5,000 young men, woman and children who were a very small cog in a big machine. The thought was that with enough pistols, we could defeat the Russians with all their power and weapons. It was certainly desperate but after thirty years we'd had enough. It felt as if it was worth the risk.

The Corvin cinema lay on one of the corners by the main crossroads in Budapest. This was the key junction which was strategically important to both Russians and Hungarians. I was a trained anti-aircraft gunner during National Service. When the Hungarian fighters heard this, they wanted me to man the machine-gun nest close to the Corvin. I had to keep explaining that there was a difference between being an anti-aircraft gunner and what they wanted. Nonetheless, I was told to defend a post that protected the Corvin. We quickly ran out of ammunition, and I was sent, along with another fighter, to return to barracks and collect more ammunition. We wanted to get as much as possible, so we hand pulled a cart. We met Colonel General Pal Maleter, the leader, and shook his hand. He congratulated us for getting this far. By the time we took the ammo it was the middle of the night, and the Soviet curfew was in place. When we tried to return to the Corvin we saw Russian tanks begin to break through one of the lines at the junctions, overrunning the defences. The other guerrilla fighter and I hid in a doorway as we saw four or five Russian tanks rumble past. In the doorway we discussed what we should do. We both came to the same decision – sod it! We dumped the ammunition and the cart and headed towards the Austrian border as fast as we could. The walk to the border took about three days, roughly 80-100 kilometres. We did manage to get the odd lift on a cart driven by oxen. We had dived into ditches when we saw cars go by in case the drivers were ARVO or communists. As soon as my colleague and I reached Austria, we split up and never saw each other again.

Goulash Soup a l'Solti

Leo made a fabulous Hungarian goulash soup. It was absolutely delicious and loved by all the family and no-one could quite seem to replicate it. The recipe was written down by Leo at some point in the past and somehow misplaced until it was recently found by George. Here is the recipe verbatim (except he spelt it 'gulyas') which serves four persons:

Ingredients:
- 1.5 lbs stewing stake cut to bright size.
- 2 large of 3 small onions cut medium.
- 1.5 lbs carrots pealed and cut to vegetable size.
- 2 lbs potatoes pleased and cut to vegetable size.
- 2 - 3 large segments of garlic (crushed).
- 200 grams (half tin) of chopped tomatoes (or fresh).
- 1 level tea spoon of caraway seeds.
- 2 level table spoons of mild/sweet paprika powder.
- 4 bay leafs (taken out when served)
- Salt, ground black pepper, chilly powder to taste.

Saute the onions in a little oil until half cooked. Add caraway seeds, paprika, chilly powder, salt, black pepper, garlic and meat.

Turn up the heat to maximum to brown the meat, turning all the time. You have to add extra oil to stop burning. When done, add water, tomatoes, bay leafs and then turn down the heat to medium/ low.

Boil until the meat is nearly done, add more water and add carrots until the carrots are nearly done.

Add the potatoes, you may need a little more water. Boil until done (do not over boil).
Top up the water - don't forget this is a soup.

(Optional - you could add a spoon full of sour cream of half a pot of natural yoghurt, 1 glass of red wine and an extra tablespoon of paprika).

Bon Appétit - Jo etvagyat.

Notes: Every Hungarian household and restaurant use different recipes - this is mine.
The collective name of the gulyas is Porkolt, which means singed or browned. Any type of meat can be used for Porkolt, chicken, lamb, mutton, beef (which is the goulash) and even fish.

You can serve it with brown rice or pasta (cooked separately) instead of potatoes (the family normally have the potato version but served with crusty bread to dip in the soup).

If you double up the meat and reduce the water then that will make a proper goulash/main course.

The wedding of Leo's grandparents Antal Emil Schmelka and Roza Knill, 07 November 1867.

Örkényi felvétel. 1916/7 16.

Leo's father (far right) in a prisoner of war camp in 1916 (possibly Siberia).

The wedding of Leo's parents Leo Karoly Schmelka and Rozalia Ilona Gaal, 18 July 1923.

Leo and his sister Magdi circa 1934.

Leo (centre) with friends circa 1935.

Leo's grandfather Antal circa 1934.

Leo outside the house he lived in Acs in the 1930s. His family occupied the bottom right quarter. Photo taken by Nick on a visit in 1999.

Leo looking very smart circa 1936.

The Corvin Cimena in Budapest which which was the strategic location Leo defended against the Russians in November 1956. Photo taken by Nick on a visit in 1999.

An iconic postcard of the 1956 Hungarian Uprising.

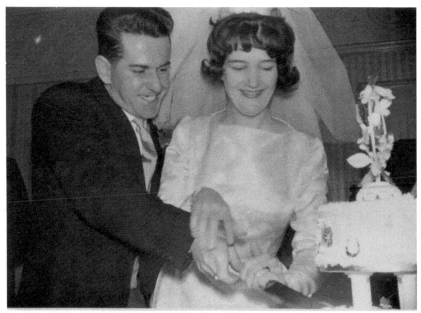

Leo and Anne's wedding 07 March 1964.

Leo looking very proud of his very first car circa 1960.

Leo, London circa 1960.

Leo's wonderful friend Janos Kovacs looking like a film star in his
Hungarian Air Force uniform circa 1942

Janos Kovacs and glamorous wife Irma God parents to Leo and Anne's children circa 1970.

Leo and beloved cousin Babus enjoyed wine and palinka at the family vineyard. Photo taken by Nick on a visit in 1999.

Leo and Bob Chiltern catching up circa 1990.

Leo after a glider flight in 2016, aged 82.

Leo's wonderful cousin Lali at his vineyard circa 1999.

Leo at Joe's and Lisa's wedding in Sorrento in 2005. Left to right George, Nick, Leo, Anne, Joe, Lisa, Charlie and Bebba with Leo's granddaughters Georgina and Jess as the bridesmaids.

The family crypt in Kunzenmarton.

Leo and Anne's 50th wedding anniversary in Rye in 2014. Left to right back row Bebba, Joe, Lorraine, Nick, and Lisa. Front row Isobel, Anne, Leo, Jess and Georgina.

Leo's grandsons Leo (junior) and Joshua 2021.

Nick, Leo (junior), Emily, Josh, Joe, and George saluting Leo with a glass of Unicum at Leo's wake in August 2019.

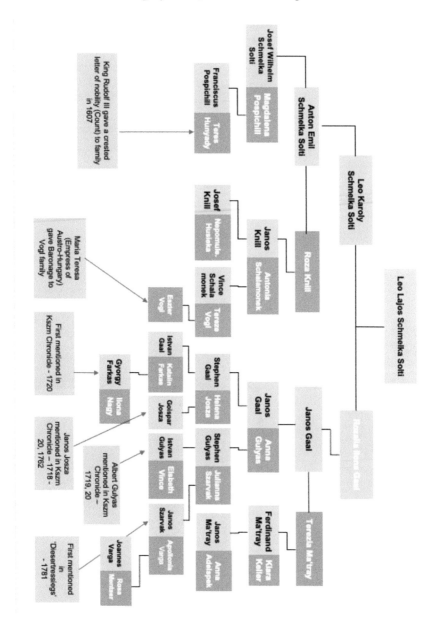

Hungary 1956, Two Worlds Apart

Generation	Name	Birth Date and Place	Death Date and Place	Marriage
1	Leo Lajos Solti Schmelka	18 Nov 1933, Gyor		1964?
2 - Parents to Leo Lajos	Leo Karoly Solti Schmelka Rozalia Ilona Gaal	3 Jun 1893, Budapest Baptised: Terézvárosi, Budapest, Pest-Pilis-Solt-Kis-Kun 1 May 1898, Kunszenmarton	7 Apr 1947, Kunszenmarton 1 May 1937, Acs	18 July. 1923
3 - Parents to Leo Karoly	Anton Email Schmelka Roza Knill	7 Nov 1867, Budapest 30 Aug. 1870, Budapest Baptised: Józsefvárosi, Budapest, Pest-Pilis-Solt-Kis-Kun (4 Sep 1870)	6 Feb 1944, Obuda 2 Mar. 1955, Budapest?	28 Aug. 1892
3 - Parents to Rozalia	Janos Gaal Terezia Ma'tray	17 May. 1838, Kunszenmarton 7 Sept 1864, Kunszenmarton	Unknown 10 Aug. 1929? Kunszenmarton	17 Jan. 1887
4 - Parents to Anton	Josef-Wilhelm Schmelka Magdalena Pospichill	30 Dec. 1831, Vienna 6 Nov. 1832, Budapest	Unknown, Budapest 25 June. 1900 Budapest	15 Aug. 1855
4 - Parents to Roza	Janos Knill Antonia Schalamonek	24 May. 1836, Skalorenc 20 Apr. 1843, Prusznitz	Unknown (77 years) 07 June. 1941, Unknown	21 Jan. 1866
4 - Parents to Janos	Janos Gaal Anna Gulyas	17 May. 1838, Kunszenmarton 17 May. 1841, Kunszenmarton	Unknown Unknown	11 Nov. 1861
4 - Parents to Terezia	Ferdinand Ma'tray Klara Keller	27 July. 1824, Csongrad Unknown	Unknown Unknown	Unknown
5 – Parents to Magdalena	Franciscus Pospichill Teres Hunyady	Unknown Unknown	Unknown Unknown	Unknown Unknown
5 - Parents to Janos K.	Josef Knill Nepomulena Husieka	1890, Unknown Unknown	Unknown Unknown	Unknown Unknown
5 - Parents to Antonia	Vince Schalamonek Tereze Vogl	1810, Unknown 1800, Unknown	Unknown Unknown	Unknown
5 – Parents to Janos G.	Stephen Gaal Helena Josza	11 Nov. 1811, Unknown 22 May. 1815	Unknown Unknown	27 May. 1834
5 – Parents to Anna	Stephenus Gulyas Julianna Szarvak	31 Sept. 1817, Unknown 17 Jan. 1819	Unknown Unknown	18 Nov. 1839
5 - Parents to Ferdinand	Janos Ma'tray Anna Adelspek	Unknown Unknown	26 Aug. 1855 Unknown	Unknown

Generation	Name	Birth Date and Place	Death Date ad Place	Marriage
6 – Parents to Tereze Vogl	Unknown Eszter Vogl	Unknown Unknown	Unknown Unknown	Unknown
6 – Parents to Stephenus Gaal	Istvan Gaal Katalin Farkas	Unknown 16 Nov. 1786, Kunszenmarton	1778, Kunszenmarton ? Unknown	Unknown
6 – Parents to Helena Jozsa	Goispar Jozsa Unknown	Unknown, Kunszenmarton Unknown	Unknown Unknown	Unknown
6 – Parents to Stephanus G.	Istvan Gulyas Elsabeth Vince	Unknown Unknown	Unknown Unknown	Unknown
6 – Parents to Julianna Szarvak	Janos Szarvak Apollonia Varga	Unknown 1775, Unknown	Unknown Unknown	Unknown
7 – Parents to Katalin Farkas	Gyorgy Farkas Ilona Nagy	Unknown Unknown	Unknown Unknown	Unknown
7 – Parents to Apollonia	Joannes Varga Rosa Mentser	1746, Unknown 1750, Csongrad	Unknown Unknown	Unknown Unknown

Chapter 7 - The Hungarian Revolution, 1956

This chapter was perhaps the most difficult for me to write so far, as there are already scores of books written on the subject, analysing the events from various points of view. Some praise the achievements of the revolution, others condemn it as the cause of the loss of a whole generation of young people as casualties and refugees, fleeing to other countries.

If somebody would look at it, someone completely detached from the events, they'd have a good laugh that those pesky Magyars (Hungarians) were never happy with their lot unless they were rioting, uprising, or creating some revolution.

If you look at the Hungarian history, it might explain a few things. The problem was that Hungary was geographically positioned at the gateway between the east and west. If anybody tried to invade the east, they had to go through Hungary like the armies of Napoleon Bonaparte when he attacked Russia, the same happened to Hitler'. The opposite way, the Mongol hoards, the Huns, and the Turks would historically have to cross Hungary and Russia was no exception. All these people had the tendency to stay in Hungary after their military goal had been achieved.

Somehow, Hungary managed to get rid of the Romans, the Huns in the Middle Ages, followed by the invading Turks. Only the mighty Danube was the reason for stopping these advancing armies continuing their journey west. The Turks stayed in Hungary for 150 years and the government was forced to relocate from Buda to Pozsony (now renamed Bratislava), the capital city of Slovakia. Hungary then occupied the western part of the Carpathian basin, the Transdanubia and the north. The Hungarian army was small and could not get rid of the Turks alone and enlisted the help of the very strong, well-organised Austrian army and together, they managed to end the 150 years occupation of the Turkish army of the Ottoman Empire. Unfortunately, the Austrians stayed in the country as a '"war bounty'. It then became part of the Hungarian/Austrian Empire under the Habsburgs as the Hungarian royal family died out.

They stayed and stayed until 1848 when the Hungarians rebelled against the Austrians and after several fierce battles, the Hungarian army was defeated and the Austrians purged the top Hungarian officers in spectacular, mass, public executions.

They stayed until the Second World War and yet again, the victorious Russians who defeated them, stayed until now, i.e., 1956. Yet another uprising of 1956 came when again, Hungary tried to get rid of the Russian occupiers.

After this long, rambling, brief (or not so brief) history lesson, I will try to write the chronological events that took place:

23rd October 1956: about 20,000 peaceful demonstrators converged to the statue of an old national hero, Josef Ben, in the mid-afternoon. The President of the Writers Union read a manifesto to the assembled crowd which demanded that the occupying Russian army should leave as well as allowing Hungary to join the UN and allow the country the freedom to choose their own government in a free election. This would be unlike previous elections where all candidates were nominated by Moskva (Moscow). The students read their own demands and the crowd chanted a patriotic poem which includes the words, "we swear, swear that we never, never be slaves again".

The crowd then cut the Communist coat of arms from the centre of the Hungarian flag and this distinctive hole in the centre of the flag became the symbol of the revolution and copied everywhere. By six o'clock the crowd had swollen to over 30,000 and were very spirited, however remained peaceful. By 8pm, the Secretary of the Communist party addressed the crowd and condemned the Writers Union and students demands which angered the crowd from this hard-line stance and the demonstrators decided to take down Stalin's 9.1 metre high bronze statue, which was erected not far from the Heroes Square (a beautiful medieval church had to be demolished previously to make room for this statue). They managed to demolish and chop up the statue with an oxyacetylene torch. By 9.30pm there was nothing left of it apart from Stalin's boot which was still fixed in place and an enterprising demonstrator placed a Hungarian flag in it with a hole in the middle to the delights of the watching crowd.

At about the same time, a large crowd formed outside the Radio Budapest headquarters which was heavily guarded by the AVO (Hungarian secret police). The flash point came when the demonstrators attempted to broadcast their demands on the radio and the rather unruly crowd was then tear gassed from one of the upper windows. Then the

AVO fired into the crowd, killing several demonstrators. A Hungarian army unit was sent by the Government to relieve the situation but the Hungarian soldiers, seeing the indiscriminate carnage to the demonstrators, tore the red stars from their caps and sided with the demonstrators.

The provoked crowd then set fire to the nearby police cars and overran a military post seizing their guns which were quickly distributed between the demonstrators. Other communist symbols were also vandalised like the stars, hammer and sickle which were fixed to most of the government buildings.

24th October 1956: During the night of October 24th, under orders from Georgy Zhukov, the soviet defence minister, Russian tanks entered the city. By noon the next day, two tanks were stationed outside the Houses of Parliament. All bridges, main roads and crossings were guarded by Russian soldiers.

25th October 1956: A mass demonstration gathered outside the parliament building where the AVO units (which were stationed on the roofs of adjoining buildings) opened fire on the peaceful crowd. The Russian soldiers returned fire on the AVO, believing they were the targets of the shooting.

It was recorded that between 24th to 29th October, there were 71 armed clashes between the AVO secret police and the demonstration. The Government collapsed, then Imre Nagy became the new Prime Minister. The revolutionaries now began an aggressive offence against the Russian and AVO units.

The demonstrations and fighting not only occurred in Budapest but started to spread spontaneously to other areas of the country. Kecskemet (a large town southeast of Budapest) had a demonstration on the 26th October and, on the order of General Gyorko, the AVO opened fire on the demonstrators. Seven protestors were shot, and organisers of the demonstrators were arrested. In another case, fighter jets strafed the people in Tiszabecske (a town just east of Kecskemet) killing 17 and wounding nearly 100.

26th October 1956: in Mosonmagyarovar (near the Austrian border) the local border guard barrack soldiers were ordered to open fire on the small, peaceful demonstration, killing and wounding some 80 people. (I have no knowledge of the exact number who were killed). I have seen a book where a photo of the dead was laid out on the pavement. In this photo, it was clear that the first 5 or 6 people were woman who makes me wonder if this demonstration was made of women only.

Nobody should be surprised that after these brutal killings, the country rose up in the revolution, trying to rid the country of the oppressors.

As I mentioned earlier, I was, at the time, working at the border to re-establish the exact line of the border between Austria and Hungary. When we first heard of the revolution, we then decided that our place was in Budapest and three of us in our team of four; the young and unattached ones, started to make our way to the capital. Only one, who was married with a young family, chose to stay behind.

Unfortunately, all trains and buses were stopped, and we had to walk with occasional lifts from lorries and horse drawn carts but we did not dare to ask the drivers of cars as most cars were owned by high ranking party officials or the AVO.

When we arrived in Budapest, a young, arm-banded woman intercepted us and quizzed us if we had any experience. We had, in the army, in our National Service days. When I told her I was with the army as an anti-aircraft gunner I was directed to the Korvin field gunner position, in spite of my argument that I was not a field gunner, and the two 'gunner' positions were very different.

The Korvin cinema was at one of the major intersections between the great boulevard and Ulloi road. This strategic point held a small bunch of defenders with two small field guns, controlling both main aspects of the intersection.

There were signs of previous battles with a disabled T54 Russian tank without its conning tower and another with a damaged caterpillar chain. Nothing happened there for the next day or two. There seemed to be a lull in the fighting so one late afternoon, Zoltan and I decided to stretch our cramped limbs after we had been crouching down by our field guns all day. Zoltan was assigned to our second gun, and we had lots of time during the long night vigils to talk and become quite good friends. This happened a few days before the expected Russian counterattack started, with the purpose of crushing this revolution. We were just a few hundred, perhaps a few thousand mainly young students, all hotheads and idealists with no army training, experience, or leadership. Armed with a few handguns, we challenged the mightiest army in the world at the time.

I would have loved to be a fly on the wall at the top Russian military meeting with all the red-faced generals when Moscow demanded an explanation about the events in Hungary. To be able to hear the accusations, excuses, and counter accusations, each blaming one another and passing the responsibility for their failings to someone else as to why a few kids with barely any weapons had managed to cause such chaos for the mighty Russian army, even for a short time.

My friend's full name was Zoltan Kapowich, a Yugoslav national with a Yugoslav father and Hungarian mother who had lived nearly all his life in Hungary and spoke the language perfectly. He was about my age and was a very intelligent and well-educated young man. I believe that only the Chinese and Japanese language is more complex than Hungarian. In England, you can judge a person's background and education by their accent, where in Hungary you can do the same with their usage of some particular words and expressions. For example, if there are a number of words that all can mean the same thing. However, only a person with an excellent grasp of the language, mostly those born in Hungary, would be able to know when to use the correct word at the correct time. This is something you cannot learn from a book and Zoltan mastered this brilliantly.

The name, Kapowich, is extremely rare in Hungary. I knew only one other person to my knowledge who was someone in my university class when I was reading meteorology. I kept quizzing Zoltan about it and after the second or third time of bringing up the subject he lost his temper and yelled, "for goodness sake, I should know my family better than you!" This language was quite a bit more common.

I caught him looking at me several times with a quizzical look on his face. When I asked him what the reason for these funny looks was, he explained that I was the spitting image of their young Yugoslav King, perhaps a few years younger. He was King Peter II, who lost the throne when Tito took over the country. He was born on the 6th of September 1923 and eventually went to live in the USA. Much later, in our trek towards the west, we met a girl also marching in the same direction who also said that I could be Peter's doppelganger or identical twin, but she thought that I was much sexier looking.

The Citadella in Budapest, I believe, was originally a Napoleonic fortification, bristling with large cannons for the purpose of defending this strategically important city. I have no idea who it was supposed to be defended from, however. Later, the Habsburgs took it over, modified it and modernised it. It was to dominate the city after the failed 1848-49 Hungarian revolution (another failed revolution). At this time, Hungary rebelled against the Austrian rulers, and this was followed by a purge of people in a bloody aftermath following the rebel's collapse. During the Second World War, a German SS regiment used it during the siege of Budapest.

In a more peaceful time, it opened up with a rather posh and expensive restaurant called The Citadel. It had a breath-taking panorama over the city from there. We went there to dine one evening with the whole family including my Sister Magdi, husband Frank, Zsananna, Lali and Babus. During our dinner, a traditional gipsy orchestra entertained us, and Anne became quite fascinated by the sound of the Cimbalom, which is a unique and unusual ancient Hungarian musical instrument. It stands on legs about waist high like a small tabletop, with rows and rows of highly stretched piano wires grouped together and with a pair of short sticks with a padded end (one for each hand). With these you would hit the groups of wires to produce a sound similar to a Pianola, but it produced an infinite variation of possible sounds.

My family had one of these instruments and Lali's parents had one too. My real mother played it perfectly, as at the time, it was compulsory for any primary school teacher to play at least one musical instrument. My mother played the harmonium as well. If I remember correctly, Anne bought an audio tape of his performance, but I have never heard her play it at home.

Lali informed me, when I asked, about the exact name of the restaurant and that it shut down a few years ago and has not reopened since. It's surprising as the views are breath-taking, especially on a clear night seeing the whole panorama of the city and for an enterprising person it could be a goldmine, especially in the tourist season despite it being outside of the city.

One late afternoon, Zoltan and I decided to walk up to the Citadella. When we got to the chosen viewpoint, it became dark. Lying on the grassy slope, we could see the last of the street lighting being switched on, district by district and we could see the pitch-black ribbon of the river Danube just below our feet. The only interruption to this blackness was the five lit-up bridges that crossed the river. Both sides of this black strip were the reflection of the lights emitting from the buildings on the Pest side. On the left, only a few hundred yards away, we could see the Margaret Bridge which led to the south end of Margaret Island. Further along the chain bridge was in view followed by the Szabadsag Bridge (Freedom Bridge) by the foot of the Gallert Mountain.

We could trace the line of the small boulevard, guided by the street lighting and also running away from us. This was the dead straight Andrassi Street into the blackness of the area of the Varosliget (city park). We could trace again the large, half circular of the great boulevard, running from the Margaret Bridge to the Petofi Bridge. Straight ahead, we could see the unmistakable silhouette of St. Stevens Basilica.

Lying there, Zoltan remarked that it was surprisingly quiet in the middle of a central European capital city in the middle of a siege. We could only hear the light hum of the traffic in the distance and just now breaking the stillness was a laborious chug-chugging of a tugboat just emerging from the side of Margaret Island, dragging three large barges downstream and eventually disappearing round a large bend towards Csepel.

The barges were fully laden, the first heavily loaded with tree trunks, obviously on their way to a sawmill. The other two, judging by the freeboard, was probably carrying bricks or other heavy building materials.

Contradicting Zoltan's remark about the apparent silence, there were suddenly two rifle shots in the distance coming from somewhere in the city park area. This was then answered with a burst of sub-machine gun fire and then a string of tracer bullets in the air which provided a pretty aerial display.

We then started to talk about our position. We realised the revolution was probably closed to being over and the Russians would never back out. The Kadar government were reportedly in discussions with the Russian delegation the possibility of withdrawing the Russian troops and armaments from Hungarian soil and then to sit down to agree the future relationship between the two countries as the occupancy and inability to join the UN had caused this in the first place. Also, another aim was to allow Hungary to have a free and fair election.

Logically thinking about the situation, you could not possibly imagine that the all-powerful Russia would give up a part of their empire to a bunch of rebellious kids and hot heads. To the Russians, this incident in Hungary was only a minor irritating flea bite. The freedom fighters were able to hold the Russians in check for a few weeks. One of the best parts was the Korvin cinema which was the crossing from the main boulevard to the Ulloi Street. The cinema was just off the crossroads and commanded a strategic position, controlling the whole area. It was manned mostly by university students, mixed up with anyone else who cared to join them. I do not know how many of them were holed up there, but I don't think it could have been more than twenty or thirty, but their numbers were swelled. It was even doubled by other freedom fighters from all over the city looking for food and shelter at night. Some of these were just kids as young as 13 years old. They managed to knock out two large T54 Russian tanks at the Boraros Square. Wedged halfway down the passageway to a public convenience and the right place for them. The defenders had two large field guns covering the intersection. The commander was a chap, Janos, with a very bad limp. I did not realise that one of his legs was made from wood and thus he was named Falabu Janos meaning 'Wood-Leg John' although this was only said behind his back.

As I mentioned earlier, lots of heroic youngsters sheltering at the Korvin at night, told us a lot of interesting stories which happened all over the city and also managed to cause a lot more headaches for the Russians. These resourceful youngsters had tricks like jumping up on the blind side of a Russian tank and planting a Hungarian flag on it and enjoying the fruits of their prank when another Russian tank would see it and blow it up.

The Russian commanders then worked out what was happening and worked out how to identify their tanks in the future.

Another trick the youngsters worked out was to entice a Russian tank into a cul-de-sac by following a captured, well-flagged army jeep with a mounted machine gun. Half-way up the street, the jeep managed to escape by using the interlocking courts and alleyways. The tank could not turn its gunning tower or manoeuvre. It would have to reverse which gave the youngsters the chance to use Molotov cocktails, placed precisely on the engine intake and when the engine was taken out and the tank canopy finally opened up, they would deal with the tank crew. Those young fools would also engage the tank on steep side roads, mainly in Buda, and hide in basement flats and cellars. They managed to pour oil on the road to stop traction of the tank treads. Girls would also take part in these antics quite often.

The ferocity of the fighting was intense and unfortunately this heroism affected the whole country. I believe there were some several hundred deaths and probably twice as many injured, but 200,000 young people subsequently had to leave the country, a whole generation. Most of those who left just wanted to be free, but there was a good number who just wanted an easier life for them and their families. A few were probably running away from a bad marriage or from paying the crippling alimony. Some criminals most likely took the opportunity to get away from the police, a number of them were even mistakenly freed by the freedom fighters. Some criminals were even freed by mistake by the freedom fighters when they opened the prisons to try and rescue politicians and other people who had been wrongly arrested.

Zoltan and I decided that the minute the Russian offensive started, using Peter and Paul our favourite ponies, we would make tracks towards freedom. We knew from experience that the punishment and reprisals would be harsh, brutal, and severe. It would also include the not-so-unfamiliar show trials shown in cinemas and written in magazines much like Cardinal Mindszenty and later, after the uprising was over, the Prime Minister Imra Nagy, Donat Ference and Paul Maletr. The freedom fighters were next on the list for these kinds of trials.

It was going on towards midnight and in our long discussion, we had forgotten the time. We were getting rather cold as we had originally set out in our T-shirts, so we made our way back to the Korvin.

The next day was rather quiet and Zoltan and I decided that we would try to get a side arm for me as I was the only one there without a gun. We marched into the city and saw a young policeman guarding the UAS embassy in Szabadsag Square (Freedom Square). He was very young, perhaps just out of police training college and very frightened when Zoltan pressed his gun against the lower part of his spine. He handed his gun over when asked. My newly acquired gun had two dummies and one live round in the magazine, perhaps showing how much the authorities trusted their own police. I felt quite safe with Zoltan as he had a fully loaded gun with live ammunition.

The following day was also quiet, and, in the late evening, we settled down on our mattresses and had just started to doze off when a very loud shout brought us from our blankets. Another shout brought us into full consciousness, followed by several others and then somebody started shooting which then escalated into full mayhem. Somebody produced a torch, and, in its light, we could see ten or so black-clad figures wearing balaclavas, descending from the windows of the flats overlooking the Korvin's large roof using short ropes. Eventually, someone shot a green rocket from a Webley pistol and in its eerie light, the picture became clear.

It seems that the Russian Commando Unit tried to dislodge us from the back as all frontal attacks were successfully repelled during previous attempts. Most of the commandos were killed but I heard a couple were wounded and captured. I had no idea whatever happened to them.

The next day, Falabu Jancsi (also known as Uncle Johnnie) called Zoltan and me to go to a large barracks with a list of supplies that were badly needed. I cannot recall the name, but it was somewhere near the city park. The list included ammunition for our guns, ordnance for the field guns as well as other items, small arms ammo, hand grenades, more blankets for the upcoming autumn nights and much needed food which we had run out of.

Food was critical as, up to now, we had managed to buy our food from the nearby shops, but they had all run out completely of any edible items and the resupply had only just begun to start. The local inhabitants were very generous, sharing their meagre food stocks with us. Later, when bakers started producing the bread, the regular supply of baked goods arrived each morning. None of it got a gold standard for cooking but it kept us going.

We had some very moving and humble experiences. For example, when an old, white-haired lady bought a small basket full of lovely, juicy red apples, perhaps the entire crop of her only apple tree, we devoured them all as we had not seen or eaten fresh fruit in many, many weeks. It took her an hour each way to walk into the city from one of the suburbs where she lived.

Similarly, a gentleman (an army officer judging from his ramrod straight back and military style moustache) gave us a dozen eggs. To his disappointment, we had to refuse them as we had no means to cook or boil them. We could not even make a cup of tea or coffee as there were no facilities. I wondered where he would keep his hens in the city, perhaps a roof garden or large balcony.

When Zoltan and I arrived at our destination with our list and hand cart, a rather stroppy, bad tempered supply Sergeant refused to give us anything at all. In the middle of our argument, a very high-ranking officer turned up and wanted to know what these civilians were doing in the barracks. When we explained our quest, he immediately ordered the shirty sergeant to not only give us all that we had requested but also to load our hand cart with help from himself.

Meanwhile, the same high-ranking officer sent us to the canteen to get some food and drink. He also shook hands with us, thanking us for our efforts and told us to keep fighting. While in the canteen, somebody pointed out that the high-ranking officer was Colonel Paul Maletr (the Commandant who became the figurehead of the fighting and, later on, the head of the negotiating team for the future of Hungary with the Russians). There were some accusations of him selling out the revolutionaries, but I don't know if these were true or not.

On the way back to the Korvin with our supplies we were about halfway there when we heard a faint but unmistakable sound of armoured cars and heavy artillery. First, we did not worry about it, but then the same sound came from yet another direction and then it got closer and obviously the tanks intended to encircle the city and we realised that the Russian offensive to crush the uprising had begun.

We then promptly dumped our hand cart in one dark alleyway, helped ourselves to some of the food and started to make our way towards our freedom. We would dodge in and out of doorways and saw some of the passing tanks, followed by some twenty to thirty rather nervous, trigger-happy Russian soldiers whose motto was, we believed to be but might be wrong, to shoot first and ask questions later.

We had to go to Zalaegerzeg first, before attempting to cross the border, as we needed the most important, up-to-date maps. I also had to sort out some outstanding arrangement and commitments and needed money as I was completely out, but luckily Zoltan had quite a lot. We were both heavy smokers and needed to buy cigarettes.

There was a lot of money in the office safe, I don't know how much, but there was enough to buy a brand-new motorbike or something similar, maybe about 800 -1000 pounds in total.

We decided that we would skirt the Balaton (the largest Hungarian lake southwest of Budapest) on the north side as it was the most direct route. Also, the roads were busier on this route which made it easier to get lifts. The Russian attack had begun in Budapest, but we thought it was still relatively safe in the countryside. The distance from Budapest to Zalaegerszeg was 224 kilometres. Lali recently informed me that he had taken this journey weekly for several years for his work. We managed quite well, thumbing lifts, and got there in the next 24 hours.

When we arrived to Zalaegerszeg we went to see my landlady, a Mrs Szabo, from whom I had rented my room as well as an extra small lock-up for the firm's measuring equipment and also my theodolite. When we turned up at Mrs Szabo's doorstep we received a very disproving look at our very poor appearance. We did not realise we had three weeks of facial hair, no haircuts for ages and had worn the same clothing for some considerable time which included no showers or baths for over two weeks. We must have looked and smelt like scarecrows rather than the heroic freedom fighters we thought we had been.

While Zoltan stripped, or rather peeled, off his clothing and got into the bath, my very stern, but really soft-hearted landlady sent for her husband and when he saw us had a really good laugh at us and handed us a stiff drink of Palinka (strong plum brandy). While this went on, Mrs Szabo disappeared to do some urgent clandestine errand. While Zoltan had a good soap and shampoo I went up to the office, which were some 15 minutes walk, to return my theodolite and other measuring equipment. It was quite a lot to carry but I didn't want to make two journeys.

The office was shut, so I believe it must have been a Saturday afternoon or perhaps Sunday, but I had keys to get in. I returned and logged off the use of the equipment and took my money out of the safe and other personal papers as well as the most important item, the secret map of the border area I had worked on previously. I had signed for these as I did not want my colleagues (who were very decent people) to get into trouble. While I was clearing up my desk, I came across an unopened letter which somehow had worked its way to the bottom of my tray and had been overlooked for some time. I instantly recognised it as having been written by my sister as I saw her stylish and unique handwriting. This letter had been sent to Pech (a large city in the south of Hungary) and then to my branch office at Zalaegerszeg. The letter informed me that I had become an uncle as she had given birth to a little girl early in August and Susan was her name. Unfortunately, because of circumstances, I never met her until 1977 when she, with her two university friends, turned up uninvited on our doorstep in England, which didn't go down too well as we had just moved house a month before as well as we had just had our fourth baby (George) who was only a few weeks old at the time.

After finishing in the office, I arrived back to my lodging and a tall young man opened the door for me who I didn't recognise. He was clean shaven, and I then realised that he was wearing my clothes and it was Zoltan who I'd never seen without a beard and with tidy hair. Of course, it explained Mrs Szabo's sudden errand who had dashed off previously to enlist the services of a retired barber who lived just round the corner from her.

My arrangement with my landlady was to do my laundry as part of the rental agreement. I was an ideal lodger who was only there for an occasional weekend and her husband often liked to chat when I was there over a glass or two of Palinka. After a very hectic and busy working life, he found his retirement boring and quite lonely. His family had all grown up and moved away and the couple would only see them at Christmas.

I squared up my rent at the time, giving an extra month's rent too. We could only carry a small number of items in our backpacks. This included underwear, an extra pullover, scarf, hat, and that was about all we could take. I asked her to take Zoltan's and my clothing to a secondhand shop as it was still worth some money.

She was in tears when we left, kissing both of us, wishing us well and good fortune and insisted that we took some of her food for our journey. Mr Szabo (Paul) insisted we took his own hip flask filled with his best, homemade Palinka. The only thing I took with me was my family ring, a fantastic Zeiss icon lens camera which I had for many years after, not just because it took excellent pictures but also the size of the picture was 24x24 not the usual 24x36. I was able to take about 44 total shots with it as a result.

The only thing that happened on our trails to the west was as we tried to avoid all villages in fear of the police, we would march on during the cover of night, lying in corners of fields or coppices for sleep. We were in trouble with very alert and vicious farm dogs on guard that detected us and only a rather sturdy stick would manage to persuade them to leave our ankles and legs alone.

One night, Zoltan misjudged the distance in the very hazy light when he tried to jump over a seemingly dry ditch and fell into some stinking mud up to his middle. When I pulled him out, amid lots of cursing, he was a terrible sight. He tried to scrape the worst of the perfumed disguise off with very limited success and had to wait till it finally dried on him when it would hopefully fall off. A few miles later, we stopped by some bushes for Zoltan to relieve himself when I heard a loud screech and more curses when he discovered when two or three large and fat leeches had attached themselves to his penis. When he took off his trousers, he then found several others had attached themselves to his legs.

I was extremely rude, but I could not help laughing at a naked man in the middle of a winter evening doing a St. Vitus dance in the moonlight with his leech dancing partners as he tried to shake off his unwanted guests. The only way to remove them was to apply salt (which we did not have) or burn them off with a lighter. His matches were already completely soaked but I still had mine, so we started the delicate proceedings in the dark to try and burn them off.

If anyone had had videoed the scene (Candid Camera/You've Been Framed) it would definitely have made £200. I could not name the style of his dance, but it was a combination of a Zulu war dance and the American Red Indians' rain dance, perhaps. Zoltan was very worried that as there was no clean water to wash the areas where the leeches had been attached but hoped the next day we would find clean water as we would be in Austria.

The day before getting to our intended destination, we spent most of the day by a largish lake and we witnessed an unforgettable spectacle. In the warm, late summer sunshine, there was a display of a dozen or so very large dragonflies flittering over the lake, while feeding on small midges and other tiny insects. It was an array of kaleidoscope colours - iridescent blues, reds, turquoise and greens. Around the edges, adding to this aerial display was the much smaller, but similarly coloured, damsel flies competing with their larger cousins.

Above the spectacle, the mill pond, like water, mirrored the colours above – I run out of superlatives here. I have never since seen anything like that and don't think I ever will.

The next day we actually arrived at the border and could see the watch towers in the distance and also saw other people going in the same direction in small groups of two or three, but also entire families from granddads to babies in mothers' arms. It was a huge exodus, and everyone's faces were clouded with fear but also with hope in their eyes.

We arrived at the border at exactly the same spot I had preselected, and we just strolled through it. It is ironic that this was the most important part of my life. I'm looking back now over six decades and have no idea when and where we actually crossed this magic line. I guess it must have been about the 10-12th of November 1956. The place or location is even more difficult to pinpoint. The largest Hungarian city close by was Lenti, which I had visited several times before when I had to buy food and cigarettes whilst working in the fields surveying the border region. This was near the 'triple point' where Austria, Yugoslavia and Hungarian borders met. It was a few kilometres south of Lenti.

I cannot recollect the name of the small Austrian village where we eventually arrived either after crossing the border. At the Austrian village, the local police wrote down our details, names, date of birth, mothers name etc. and promptly confiscated our side arms and took the most up-to-date maps in current existence.

That night the temperature dropped some 12 degrees, and our Austrian hosts were surprised to see this unseasonable and early arrival of the hard frost.

We were homed at the local primary school with camp beds and mattresses on the floor. We were given the Austrian version of the Hungarian goulash with "Nokedly" which is a type of pasta/dumpling, and this was extremely welcome as we had not seen cooked food for quite some time.

The very next day, a very official looking gentleman came who was dressed in a three-piece white suit. My father used to have these stiff and starched colours, they were extremely uncomfortable, especially in the summer heat waves, but he still wore them his entire working life. This man also wore a monocle in his eye and was accompanied by an interpreter. He was looking for 'the chap with those highly confidential maps. He asked me how I had come into possession of these and when I explained the reason he departed, seeming to be satisfied with my answer.

I understood that there was something on my maps that interested the Austrian authorities. I believe, even the American intelligence service was also interested. I happened to be an innocent courier of this information - whatever it was.

The next day he returned with yet another official who spoke some passable Hungarian. During the conversation/interview, I boasted that I could cross the border blindfolded. They asked me if I would be prepared to go back again and collect as many fleeing refugees as possible and guide them back across the border. I realised that I really should have kept my trap shut - shouldn't I?

The authorities were worried that, before too long, the border guards would return, and the crossing would once again be impassable. I agreed to their request, and I set out on my first foray to collect some 70-80 scared refugees, guiding them successfully across the border. The following night, there was over a hundred people and as the exodus of bodies increased the going became very difficult as the very hard frost overnight made ploughed fields difficult to negotiate it being mainly at night and at dusk.

The next day it was warm and sunny. The temperature must have been at least 18-20 degrees. However, when the sun went down, the temperature would drop sharply which created a dense fog everywhere. On my expedition that night, I saw people had gotten lost and were running in every direction and had become confused and panicking, running back towards Hungary. I myself, knowing the landscape intimately, had to keep all my wits about me to find my way. In that night, I collected another 80-90 people and took them to safety.

I was desperately tired from the nights of expeditions and little sleep. I was starting to dream of a night of undisturbed and full sleep. The next day's duty, unfortunately, called again and I started to get ready for another night's work of human transportation. I must have had some kind of premonition about this as I remembered I took with me some family photos for the first time ever. Everything started well and so far, this was the biggest group of fleeing and frightened people I had led to safety. We were just about to cross the border when the quiet night was suddenly shattered into bedlam. Noise from sub-machine guns from the right-hand tower close by rang out and I assume this was from the Russian border guards who had returned. People were fleeing in all directions, mothers separated from their lost and crying children. Babies were crying and the wounded were screaming in pain for help. To make all of this more frightening the harsh searchlight beams were probing the darkness and also there were several small explosions from the guards who were now throwing hand grenades. I was hit by a bullet in my upper arm which was a bit painful, and I also felt a lot of blood running from my arm, it made my hand rather sticky with it. I kept going as I knew I was less than a hundred foot from my goal. The second bullet hit me in the shoulder, a searing pain gurgled in my chest, and I was starting to bleed profusely but I still managed to continue crawling forward, but it was getting more and more difficult. Finally, less than 25 feet from the border I started to lose consciousness. Lying there, semi-conscious, I was still able to move my head from side to side and as I looked up, I could see a magical scene. If it was not for the deadly serious nature of the situation, it would have been beautiful. In the darkness, the lights were probing around, and the snow began to fall. They looked like small powder puffs or pieces of candy floss, flying in the wind and it seemed wondrous when mixed with the search lights from the guard towers.

In my slowly clouding mind, my brain seemed to be still functioning and I suddenly realised I was dying. I surprised myself that I felt no fear of this. I was lying prone on the frozen, hard ground and was feeling extremely cold, no longer able to move or feel my fingers, hands, or legs. Partly because of the frost but also, more likely, due to the blood I was rapidly losing.

Apart from the pain from the wounds, I was conscious about the pain on my right hip. When I hit the ground, I assumed I had fallen on a brick or stone but none of those were anywhere.

It must have been a small tree stump sticking out of

the ground when the trees and saplings were cut back to provide firewood for the guards. I was thinking that it must be about my birthday and thought, if so, I would be in good company as my mother died on her 31st birthday so why not me on my 23rd. Then shortly after that, everything went fuzzy and then black.

The Great (Hungarian) Escape

I was hit twice, and I remember being dragged and hauled across the border. Nonetheless, I made it. I didn't completely lose consciousness at the time of the shooting, but I did lose a lot of blood and shortly passed out after that. I know it must have been bullets from a machine gun that hit me because the bullet holes lodged a few inches from my heart. I'm not sure I would have made it if the bullets had come from rifles, they would have passed straight through me!

Chapter 8 – I'm in Heaven

I am floating in a warm, light and friendly cloud in complete silence and stillness. I am free of any pain apart from a slight discomfort from my chest and my right hip is still slightly sore, perhaps just to remind me that what had just happened only a very short time ago was not just a bad dream.

When I eventually and reluctantly opened my eyes, I saw a tall, blonde angel standing by my side, bending over and she said something to me which I did not understand. Then, when my brain started to function a little better and I started to ask myself "why is my angel wearing a nurse's uniform?" Suddenly it dawned on me that I was in a hospital and my angel was a nurse.

Earlier, I was taken by ambulance from the border area to the hospital in a suburb of Vienna where they removed the two bullets. One from my chest and the other from my arm and gave them to me as a souvenir. I thought I brought them to England with me, but I had lost them at some point. They were probably the same size as the diameter of a pen and about an inch long, if they had been rifle bullets that had hit me I would have been killed.

One of the bullets had hit me and finished up only half an inch from my heart. They put me on a drip and generally patched me up.

During my recovery period in the hospital, I received several visitors, which was very interesting and gratifying. One of those visitors was the two Austrian gentleman who had persuaded me to undertake the nightly excursions back to Hungary. They told me that I had helped over at least 300-400 people to cross safely to Austria.

The other two people visiting me were the two chaps who saw me, semi-consciously lying on the ground and still tried to crawl, crab-like, a few feet from the border and together, they managed to drag me over the 'magic line'. One of the other visitors was a reporter or something like that. After she heard my story, as I recited by my bed, and after having my story verified by the others, she said, "you deserve a medal for what you have done".

I stayed in hospital for a week or ten days and was then taken to a refugee camp by coach, somewhere near Linz. The refugee camp was quite large compared with other, previous camps I'd visited which had makeshift huts, hastily divided into small cubicles which slept two in each. They were of timber construction and hardboard nailed to them with no paint in sight. The furniture consisted of one chair – the lower bunk was the other chair. Hooks were provided to hang our clothes from, and the ceiling and the door was a piece of heavy-duty canvass and the floor was concrete and had rush matting (a small luxury) but even those were not even in the prime of their lives. The lighting was a single, dingy bulb hanging in the middle.

Each cubicle had a window but half of them were so badly fitted or corroded they could not perform the function they were designed for.

It was late autumn and early winter was upon us and it was very cold, under two degrees, very stiff army blankets and straw filled mattresses and army pillows that were nearly as smelly as the ones in the national service places in Hungary. I cannot recollect the heating arrangements, but I imagine it was frugal and minimalistic in nature.

In these huts, I guess they must have housed about over 100 people with a long central corridor and cubicles on either side and at each end were half a dozen toilets, basins and two shower cubicles with a spasmodic supply of hot water. This added up to one shower cubicle for fifty people.

As we are in the theme of 'I am in Heaven', this new camp was incomparable. It was located in one of Linz's suburbs and we could walk into the city within half an hour. Perhaps the same distance that our house at Angmering Lane is to the Rustington shops. The camp was on the ground of a disused area. Looking at the austerity of the layout and the typical armed forces barracks and one more upgraded one which was perhaps the officer's mess or quarters. There were two or three multi-story buildings surrounding a central square, perhaps the old parade ground. We were housed in one of the large three-story buildings. According to the mid-to-late 1950s social ethics, the male and female sexes were strictly segregated. Two thirds or three quarters of the refugees were male, and this is why we were put in one of the larger buildings. The women were put up in one of the smaller buildings and away from the men.

The individual units had linoleum-covered floors, lockable doors with plenty of room like a more modern, small hotel room. It included two divan beds with a drawer underneath with our meagre luggage which was lost in these drawers. Apart from the beds there were two chairs, bedside cabinets and small hanging wardrobes which also served as a writing desk. In one corner was a wash basin with mirrors. Good-sized radiators under the windows which looked out onto the grounds – i.e., Heaven!

The rooms were decorated in pastel colours and the doors were painted in contrasting, rather sharp colours. Reds, greens, and blues. This was rather interesting as I'd never seen this type of decoration but once you got used to it, I liked the concept.

The beds were pure luxury after the straw-filled, lumpy mattresses we had previously lain on. The thought of being 'In Heaven' seemed to continue as we had a proper sprung mattress, proper pillows, sheets, and duvets on the beds. Some of the walls even sported some pictures as well as curtains in the windows, bedside light and even a radio. Ablutions were shared between four or five rooms and had showers with constant and hot running water.

Canteen facilities were housed in a separate building which looked and felt more like a restaurant rather than an army canteen where large amounts of unappetising food were slapped on our plates by the harassed canteen staff.

Although we had to get our food from the buffet, there was plenty of selection and choice. We still had to carry our tray to the table of our choice, but the tables were always clean and cleared of previous use and had white Dumask table clothes with knives and forks etc. laid out for us with large jugs of water and condiments waiting for us. Even toothpicks were there, which at the time, were essential items on the dining table.

While we were enjoying our time there, we were taken by coach loads to a central office to be registered and 'interrogated' by officials. The interrogation was not the type you could see in the war films but a friendly, business-like interview around a desk and everything was meticulously written down with Germanic fastidiousness. I noticed in my interview that they opened up the file on me and there were all the hand-written notes from the previous interviews which were taken by the police when we registered originally in the village after crossing the border in Austria.

I noticed an interesting technique during these 'interrogations. Questions were asked about you, details of grandparent, primary school, grammar, university, how you spent your summer holidays, which courses were taken. This could be learnt in parrot fashion and when the questions would be fired at you in rapid bursts by two or three officers and after an hour or so of intensive questions, they would call a smoke/coffee break which was very welcome. One of the interviewers claimed they did not understand Hungarian, but I could tell on his face he understood some of the questions before they were translated. This informal and relaxed chat was when you would lower your guard. If you got anything to hide, funnily enough, the same technique was used where the questions in England and two subsequent interviews, one in Slough where I was also questioned on two separate times also at Egham police station when I applied for my naturalisation papers. (Which my very rude children called my 'neutralisation' papers!)

Returning to our luxurious accommodation, the upper floors also had parquet flooring, and a Persian rug in the middle of the room. If my theory is correct, the original purpose of this building was to house some very high-ranking army officers. The entrance to the block was through a pair of ornate, very large doors into a hall with marble floor covering and opposite these doors was a very large, circular picture, some 1.5 metres in diameter and in an equally ornate, carved wooden frame covered in Gesso and gold leaf. The name of the picture was the birth of Venus by Sandro Botticelli, a Florentine painter, and the original of it hangs in the Uffitzi gallery in Florence. This version shows a fully grown, naked blonde woman, with very long, wavy hair emerging from a gigantic seashell. Venus is completely naked and only her very long hair covers her rather, voluptuous, womanly curves.

My special interest in the picture was that we had exactly the same picture with a very elaborate, golden painted frame at home, hanging above my father's large desk with the exception that our Venus was not an oil painting but a petit poi (needle work) which took my mother nearly a year to complete. She did such a perfect job with it that it won several prizes which was also her pride and joy.

The Austrian Red Cross arranged to pay for a barber to come in and give us a badly needed haircut. I was ok at that point as I had mine done before we left for the border a few weeks before. It felt like it was months ago as so much had happened since then. After these various interviews, our camp was split up and segregated the people by the choices of their final destinations. Those who were still undecided, stayed there a bit longer at the camps, but the majority of us who knew where they wanted to go, were divided up.

I knew that I wanted to go to England and nowhere else. The decision was based on stories retold and by my nagging father who spent half a year scholarship education at Cambridge (and then half a year at Berlin). What intrigued me was the rather quirky habits of an Englishman, like drinking lots and lots of tea with milk? In Hungary, we would have one cup of tea in the mid afternoon with a bit of lemon juice or possibly rum on a cold winter day - NEVER, however, with milk. Naturally, the rum was only for medicinal purposes – Ha Ha! I liked the Englishman's, stiff upper lip attitude, love of sport and sportiness, general even temper and loved the constitution, the democracy and generally law-abiding way of life. The only thing I did not think sounded impressive was their cuisine. However, this seemed to be a minor price to pay for a new life and a place to spend the rest of my days.

We were actually interviewed several times, but I don't know by whom. They were certainly officials, possibly Secret Service. They wanted to know all about me, my family and my history including my parents, why I had been in Hungary and why I had tried to leave and even the names of dogs we had owned. All my answers were written down. The following day I was questioned with the same questions all over again. Funnily enough, when I was interviewed several years later about becoming a naturalised British citizen (about 1967), the questions were very similar!

Once the questioning had finally ended, we were transported to an airport, shuffled onto an old DC-3 Dakota, until it was full and then flown to England. During the flight they offered me a drink which looked like a cup of weak coffee. It wasn't coffee. It was the first time I tried a cup of tea with milk, and it made me feel sick. We landed at Blackbushe airport, in Hampshire and taken by bus to Aldershot barracks which were empty as the Army were currently in Suez dealing with the crisis there.

We were at the barracks for about a couple of weeks. We slept in comfortable bunk beds, we were served army meals three times a day and were allowed to roam the camp when we wanted. There was no specific Hungarian network that I came across, but there was even a job centre in the camp, or labour exchange as it was known, complete with an interpreter and we were offered jobs. None of us spoke a word of English. The interpreter showed us pieces of equipment relating to the type of work relating to the job on offer, for example pieces of milling machines. We were asked to nod if we knew what they were and what to do with them and, ultimately, given the job. At this point we didn't care what the job was. The most important thing was to get a job. I told them that I had been an Ordinance Surveyor in Hungary. The role was slightly different here in England and so initially they put me down as a Map Maker, which I couldn't actually do. This was eventually cleared up and the role was eventually adjusted to Draftsman and Structural Engineer.

My interview for this role was pretty comical. I was given an English/Hungarian translation dictionary. I would look up a word, point at it to the interviewer, who would either nod or shake his head in agreement. In the same manner, he would look up another word, point at it and show it to me. I would nod or shake my head. Remarkably, I got the job with Girlings Faroe Concrete Ltd based at

London Airport. I stayed with them for eight years, being promoted to Senior Designer.

When I started with Girlings, the Women's Voluntary Service (WVS) found me some accommodation. It was a spare bedroom with an English family, Ray, and Pat Hodgkins with their young child. They had asked for a Hungarian girl so that their young son (Tim) could have a playmate, but all that was on offer was me! I stayed with Ray and Pat until 1964. Ray died many years ago and I went to Pat's funeral in October 2015, she was 95. They were my mentors and my friends. Sadly, Tim died in his thirties. I was 23 and I'd just arrived in a new country where I couldn't speak the language. I was disorientated and frightened, I didn't know anyone and didn't have a thing to my name. When I first arrived in England, everything seemed so impressive, everyone seemed like millionaires. The standard of living was amazing to me.

With this, I close my 'I am in heaven' chapter (at last); a long way away from lying, bleeding, and dying on the Austrian border, before arriving to my new 'heaven' - England.

"Are you sure you want titpaste?"

While I was still at the barracks, we would often see English civilians who'd come out of kindness and goodwill to socialise. They'd play table tennis with us or take us out for a drink. I was often asked for a drink or a coffee at their house which was local.

There was one occasion where I was invited back to a Prefab, where the first thing I was shown was the loo. It baffled me for ages. This seemed very strange, surely, they'd put the kettle on first of all. It was only after I was living with Ray where he explained that this was the polite thing to do in England so that you knew where it was, and you didn't have to ask when you needed it. I wrote home to my family about this strange English custom, and they found it all very peculiar too!

I remember barbers cutting our hair for free and the local cinema wouldn't charge us. We'd sit right up at the front and, although I couldn't really understand what was being said, I generally figured it out.

Trying to understand certain English words was really difficult. My landlords, Ray, and Pat tried their level best to describe and translate more intimate or colloquial words like 'Bloody' and 'Fuc*ng' by using Latin and French! It was a nightmare. I wanted to improve my English, so started an evening class. Pat and Ray encouraged me to speak the language, dropping me off in Staines so I could manage my own shopping. I went to Boots one morning to buy some toothpaste and asked the lady for some 'Titpaste' and she replied, "Are you sure you want titpaste".

When I left Girlings I went to work with Marley's, located in Sevenoaks, it was the second of three jobs that I had. I had married Anne Collins and my daughter, Bebba, had just been born. I can't recall the first time I met Anne but had move out of Ray and Pat's and was sharing a house with Peter and John. Peter was invited to a nurses' party in Chertsey. All three of us went along (well, who wouldn't!) and it was there that I met Anne. She was with someone else at the time. Funnily enough, we talked and danced, but didn't really hit it off. We met again, six months later, quite by chance, bumping into each other at Richmond Castle, a huge dance venue with a live orchestra.

Perhaps it was the atmosphere or the music. Whatever it was, we hit it off this time and began courting many times in the next few months. As I like to say, that was the end of me!!

Continuing a Hungarian pastime

I may have left Hungary, but quite by accident, I discovered that I enjoyed and was good at, fencing. It was an incredibly popular sport when I was young and until the uprising. Hungary, along with the Italians, were at the forefront of the sport.

As a Hungarian, perhaps fencing was in the blood. Visiting France on holiday the early 1990s, I met a French fencing instructor for a lesson and caught the bug (Anne was at a silk painting lesson). He didn't speak English and taught me by acting and miming the thrusts and parries. I realised that I wanted to continue this as a hobby and, once we got home, Nick found a club in Chichester, and I joined the following week.

I competed against different clubs, in different events and as part of a team as well as individual events including foil, sabre, senior wins (over 65) and the Sussex Invitation. I have about 10 trophies where I came first, second or Runners Up. What makes it all the sweeter is that most of my competitors were pretty young.

I don't fence anymore, but still teach and train youngsters once a month, passing on the tradition.

I began gliding when I was in my teens, flying 10 different aircraft in as many years, logging at least over a hundred hours of flight. I also completed 3.5 examinations before I had to leave the country. I picked it up again, visiting a few clubs in Surrey when I initially arrived in England, but it was too expensive.

One night, returning from fencing, I saw gliders above Tangmere airfield near Chichester. Out of the blue I stopped in and explained what I'd flown in Hungary. I was offered an instructor's job on the spot by the Air Commodore who offered me a flight in a glider I'd never flown before. I took the glider up, flew a standard circuit and on finals carried out the best landing I'd ever done. The Air Commodore was suitably impressed, offering me the job again. Unfortunately, the job included training Air Cadets at the weekend. This was a huge commitment on top of family and work. Although I didn't take the role, I told the Air Commodore that he must have been mad to let me, a total stranger, in a plane worth thousands of pounds. He said that were it not for the landing, he wouldn't have offered me the job.

What would things have been like if I stayed in Hungary?

It's a tough question. If I'd have kept my head down in Hungary, under the radar, so to speak, it's interesting to think what might have happened. I would have had a different family and a good pension, but that opportunity wasn't open to me at the time. I had no choice but to move countries at the drop of a hat at the age of 22.

Chapter 9 – Reflections: Half-way House

It has been about 20 months since I started to write this story and I think it's time to stop, take stock and reflect on the work done so far and perhaps make plans for the second half.

I believe I am more than halfway through my life story and have definitely finished the Hungarian side and as the book's sub-title states, "Two worlds, Hungary and Beyond" I now endeavour to start on the 'Beyond' section.

The idea to start writing down my story all began at my granddaughter, Georgina's Christening party in September 1997 when, with a full glass of wine in my hand, I was strolling around Bebba and Charlie's garden and began a conversation with their best friend, Geoff Thorpe, who also had a well-charged glass of some nectar in his hand.

He asked me how I managed to get out of Hungary in 1956 after the Russians had crushed the revolution. When I sketched out the events to him roughly, he said it was an extremely interesting story and said "Why not write a book about it?"

The idea had never occurred to me. Perhaps I had never thought it was interesting enough to anyone, not even the family and it was totally ridiculous idea for me to write a book. I'm a technical man and not a wordsmith which has always been Anne's forte who can dress up and dramatise mundane events to make an interesting read. The second "prompt came from Hugh, Anne's nephew, who had already successfully published his first book, Spirit of the Blue" about a Battle of Britain fighter pilot and he may be thinking about the possibility of a second one. (Sorry Hugh if I stole the thunder and did it myself, with quite a lot of help of course).

After a belated family Christmas lunch in 2015 came the third nudge. Charlie and I were sitting at the end of our dining table after consuming Anne's enormous Lasagne. We were still eating stilton and biscuits, downed with port and with the frequent recharging of glasses. Charlie started asking about my escape from Hungary, just as Geoff had done. He said something that stuck in my memory although I don't recall the words precisely, "Georgina has the right to know what her grandfather had been up to". At that point I wasn't sure if that was Charlie or the port talking. I also didn't really think at the time that Georgina (or anyone else) would be interested in it.

The fourth and final push came from the family a few months later where we were sitting in our lovely, sunny, sun lounge after our family Easter lunch (another massive lasagne). I believe it was Easter Monday and after the traditional Easter egg hunt which the younger grandchildren, always enjoyed, I remember Nick, young Leo, Joe, George and Bebba sat there nagging me although, looking back, they never really nagged me; just tried, perhaps a bit forcefully, to get me writing.

After agreeing, I tried to write it on the computer using my two fingers to type and also managed to lose more than a month of work which George never managed to retrieve. After that, George came round to correct major grammatical errors as well as spell checking and even bought me a special keyboard with extra-large keys to help. After a month of work, I suddenly lost everything again and George said he had, "never seen it happen on a computer before like that or ever since". After this hiccup, we decided that I would dictate the text to George who would put in on the computer, the dictation mostly whilst down the local pub over a couple of ciders.

At the time I did not realise the tremendous amount of work that was to come. Writing is probably the easiest and quickest part, but going through it, correcting it, sometimes two or three times, before I could even begin dictating to poor George to put it on the computer – well, I'm not exactly bosom pals with IT technology (in other words I'm a complete and utter moron and IT illiterate).

George would then print the dictated work out in double line spacing which I would correct and correct again until I could return it to him to spell checked and adjustments made and proofread. Sometimes, these checks turned out so poorly that the whole chapter had to be re-written as I am doing this now with Chapter 8.

George and I sometimes carried out the dictation in a quiet corner of the lovely pub garden, the 'Sea View' nearby when the weather was good. Well-lubricating his 'computer fingers' and my vocal chords with a pint (or three) of Stowford Press cider or George's more recent tipple of Guinness. In inclement weather, we would move to the Clock House pub, a few hundred yards around the corner and the cider brand would change to a rather unusual 'Angry Orchard', which is an imported American brew. Now it's been replaced by the equally lovely Mortimer's cider.

It was not very easy for George, even while he was still living with us, to find time for this work. He is often and regularly, sent to various RAF stations to train others with computers and update data on versions of aircraft or helicopters and is often away for several days or full weeks even.

I must pay the highest tribute to George, as without his time, computer expertise and patience, all this would not be possible. May it last a bit longer (maybe quite a bit longer?). I mentioned earlier that George's time spent on this manuscrypt was at a premium, but now even more critical as Leanne and George purchased their first home of a later Victorian house, which takes every minute of their spare time to fix up and modernise.

I must also give a lot of thanks to Lali (Lulli – Ha ha!) who helped regarding my earlier life and shared experiences during the war years in Kunszentmarton. He also answered hundreds of my questions which sometimes he had to look up on the internet, doing research to provide further detail for my book.

My story is 90% as true as I can remember, but the other 10% is made up of exaggeration and poetic licence. Not that I'm claiming to be a poet – far from it. Everything I have written is true, but not necessarily as accurate as I'd like, as I'm looking back through the curtain of time of some 70 years and trying to force my tired, worn-out old brain to remember and recollect details of my early life. Especially, when sometimes they were not even that significant and try to bridge the gaps in between them.

In those early days, when family virtually demanded me to start writing, Nick very enthusiastically declared that if we could not find a publisher for the book the family will club together to publish it privately.

I know that this book is rather unusual, even mad, and rather free-spirited. Because of this, I feel that I can make up my own rules and interrupt the story with this half-way house chapter. George suggested this should be a preface, but I rejected the idea, as this chapter includes parts of a preface, the usual acknowledgments, usual excuses and disclaimers and prologue in one.

George was concerned about length of chapters but that was determined by the events that took place so one may just be ten pages or another 50 plus. I'm not playing by the rules, am I?

I am trying to contact all the people, family, friend, and neighbours and ask them if they are happy to use their names. If not, I will try to give them new names and identities. So far nobody has objected as I told them it will all be written "warts and all". Anyone who does object may be given a stupid name or character ☺.

The family had apparently lost interest in it, and nobody ever phoned, or in person ever asked, "by the way, how is the book getting on?" I had more interest from Lali and Zsuzsa, who will be most unlikely to read this, as I'm not prepared to translate it to Hungarian. Sometimes things were not going well (which happens frequently); the weather outside was rainy and gloomy, cold, the garden without a single flower, even regular garden birds were hiding or emigrated, and I felt depressed. I looked for a tinny of cider and for the slightest excuse to drop this project for good and go back to my gardening.

Dropping back to the lack of interest or disinterest comment about my family - I must correct it as Charlie did ask me once, "How is the book progressing?" The most hurtful is Anne's complete utter lack of interest and support. When I am sitting in the sun lounge and formulating the next chapter in my head, I am supposed to be 'space-watching' – although of course, I do doze off quite often.

When I finished the first chapter and George managed to print it off, I proudly gave her a chance to read it first which contained 25 odd pages, but her answer was that she didn't have time to read that now. I left it on the table to be read later. Several weeks later, I said something about the second chapter being complete and, on this prompt, she picked up Chapter One, read it briefly, and after a few minutes said something like, it is all wrong, this should be a past participial, and not something else which was lost on me. I know she is obsessed with English grammar, but I thought she may be interested in my earlier life, mainly in Hungary, as I was interested in hers.

After this long moan, I definitely feel much better and will now try to concentrate on Chapter 9.

I am at a crossroad now. Shall I pack it all in, due to the family's complete disinterest, or carry on for my own satisfaction, as I hate incomplete projects or work!

Last Sunday, Nicky came over and surprisingly asked me how the book was progressing. It seems that apart from Hugh, not only following the story, but he is right up to date with it to the point where George had managed to put it into the computer. This revived my drooping spirit, so I decided to carry on writing.

The first time I was able to read through my story so far was when I proofread it as one continuous piece, rather than one fragmented chapter at a time. George had printed out the whole lot (Chapters 1-5) and bound into one copy which I'd asked him to do as a Christmas gift. I found that it was very pleasing to read, and the story jelled quite well. It is not a 'page turner' but made a reasonable read.

I have absolutely no idea what caused the sudden change of heart with my family and the book, but it has given me enough encouragement to battle on. As I come to the end of the Chapter, it has been great to read back and see if anything has been left out, or in need of, major alteration. I'm not sure what to do with the rest of the book. I cannot have a "Three quarter-way House" chapter, because that would be TEDIOUS!!

Chapter 10 – Aldershot and Fleet

As refugees, the officials had arranged for us to be taken to a location as a temporary measure, until they could work out what to do with us.

From BlackBushe aerodrome, we were taken by coach to one of Aldershot's army barracks, called 'The Beaufort', which was located on the edge of Aldershot whose normal occupiers were at the Suez Canal, as a response to what was called the Suez Crisis if I recollect correctly. Egyptian president Nasser wanted to nationalise this international waterway and threatened to close it to shipping as all our goods going towards the east and the Indias, where Britain was still doing a large volume of trade. Interestingly, I first met one of my colleagues when I worked for Marley at Storrington much later. It was a chap called Jim Cooper who was parachuted down there while doing his National Service stint.

The barracks was very old, it may even have been built in the late Victorian era, with its long wooden huts for accommodation and a large central canteen and recreation room. I believe that it was the time when Britain had just come out of food rationing and a Post-War utility system was put in its place at Christmas. I do not recollect seeing a single Christmas tree anywhere in the barracks or in the houses, in spite of it being the Christmas season.

A life in the barracks could easily have been described in one word – BORING!!! Apart from the times of three meals a day, there was nothing to do all day apart from walking into the town in about ten minutes. We could window shop, but even the shops were very austere, perhaps this is not the right word, but it felt like the right one. With very little money we couldn't buy much. We had some dole-money, just enough to buy some Woodbine cigarettes which were the cheapest brand available. We could buy letter writing materials and postage stamps as most of us tried to write home to reassure our families that we were OK, but with no permanent address we could not expect replies for the time being.

I must say that the town's people were extremely kind and generous and very sympathetic towards us. Barbers would give us free or half-price haircuts and in the early afternoon when the cinemas were only half full, the usherettes would let us in free. During some of these cinema visits, we had some embarrassing moments when during the interval, they would show the pictures of the fighting and uprising in Hungary and a bucket was passed up and down each row of seats and everyone would put in some money for the poor refugees, and we would just have to pass the bucket on without providing any donations.

Some of us were invited to the pub in the early evenings for a glass of beer. However, I wasn't one of those lucky recipients☹. Back at the barracks in the recreation hall, there was a table tennis table with bats and balls, but all the balls were broken or split, and we could not afford to replace them. There was also a dart board with terribly blunt darts, and we had no idea how to score. We also had a black and white television set with an internal aerial which had to be fiddled with all the time to make it at all watchable. It must have been the rugby season as we could see dozens of burly men rushing at each other and sometimes would lean into the other team and try to push their opponents off their feet and kicking the ball backwards all the time, instead of the way they actually wanted to go. It was all very strange and we had no idea what the rules were supposed to be.

The only relief came in the early evenings or weekends when lots of local young men and girls came to the camp to try and teach us some basic English, but they were also very curious Magyors (Hungarians). They were mainly students of the same age group as us. During these visits, we managed to get some idea using not just oral means but also mimicking skills, like playing charades, to try and overcome the language barrier. They tried to explain the basics of rugby rules, leaving out the finer points of it. One of those young men who came in nightly to teach us English was a chap called Colin Moreton and he lived with his parents less than 200 yards from Beaumont. The parents had a small corner shop at 20, Alexander Road, using their living room as the shop and dining room as the living area and sold decorating materials. All the walls were full of paints, mainly Dulux and Dulight, paints with various colours, paintbrushes, sugar soap, sandpapers and also books of wallpaper swatches were available to order in for customers. In the back yard they had a Morris traveller, exactly the same as we used to have, except theirs was green and ours was black.

I spent hours and hours scraping the top layer of the car's wood panelling which had gotten rotten and had to be re-varnished. Mr. Morton used his car to deliver paraffin to dozens of clients weekly as, at the time, central heating was very rare, and electricity was too expensive. Everyone had one or two of these cylindrical paraffin heaters and would take them into the actual rooms where they were needed the most.

Some people got a luxury or extravagance of being able to afford to keep them on all night in the hallways to keep the chill at bay and would keep the doors partly open to heat bathrooms and other smaller rooms. Each of those clients had their own cans or containers which we had to refill from a forty-gallon drum which was put on a small platform, so an ordinary water tap would be able to fill the containers ready for delivery.

One day, Colin asked me and Paul, who I had become quite friendly with in the camp, to spend Christmas with his family which we gratefully and greedily accepted and moved into their spare double bedroom with large double bedstead. I had never shared a bed with another man before and found it quite uncomfortable. One day, I accompanied Mr. Morton on his delivery services and met a lot of interesting people.

I assumed the invitation was just for Christmas, but we did not see any decorations, Christmas tree or Christmas dinner whilst sitting round the table of the Moretons' on Christmas day. They tried to teach us some basic words by pointing to things on the table - a plate, knife, spoon, or fork etc. In return, for fun, they asked us to tell them about the equivalent in Hungarian. It was going quite well until somebody pointed to the cheese, when we said the cheese was 'Sajt' (pronounced shite). Everyone was hooting with laughter as we both looked very baffled, they explained/mimed by holding their noses in one hand and pretending to pull the lavatory chain with the other.

Whilst staying there, Mrs Morton's brother came over and took us on a mini pub crawl, introducing us to their friends and asked us into their prefab home which they made very homely and also sat down with a cup of tea, immediately pointing out that the location of the WC was upstairs. I found the gesture was rather puzzling until someone explained that we could relax and not get embarrassed to ask where 'IT' was when we needed to go.

When we got back to the barracks the evacuation was in full swing and we were moving to another camp in Fleet as the rightful occupiers of the barracks had begun arriving home after the successful completion of the Egyptian / Suez Canal campaign.

Fleet

The Fleet Camp was more recent or newer than Beaumont Barracks, with rows and rows of huts which all seemed to be much roomier than the previous ones. The main buildings were updated and purposeful. For example, there was a large recreation area where the Camp Commander organised dances on Saturday nights with up-to-date gramophone records to dance to.

There was also a 'Job Centre', or labour exchange, which offered lots of vacancies. The way it worked was that due to the language difficulties, the official showed us an enlarged photograph like a milling machine, lathe, or similar machinery, and if the applicant nodded in a positive way, they would arrange an interview for him with the factory foreman. If he was happy, the job was yours, subject to finding suitable lodging's nearby.

I realised that the present climate of 'trying to help those poor Hungarian refugees' would not last forever, only until a more newsworthy event took place for the news hungry media to feed on and they would forget about us. I was one of the first the following morning to take advantage of this facility. Unfortunately, when they filled up my card to the question of my occupation, they could not translate 'Ordnance Surveyor' so they finished up with a 'Mapmaker/Draftsman'. In the meantime, they actually sent me up to London to the National Geographic Society for a job interview which, of course, was a total waste of time, money, and effort.

On the second or third day at the Fleet Camp, someone recognised me from the 'Bush Telegraph' and several people came to talk to me and shake my hand. I even got a hug or two from people I helped through the Austrian border. One of them, in a group of seven, I had already noticed as they stayed together all the time and had a wide variety of ages. As it turned out, I had helped them cross the border the night before the border was closed down and, if I remember correctly, it was the night when the dense fog had blocked out all possible directional indicators and I actually carried one of the twins in the group, but I could not recollect his name. We became quite friendly, and he told me they decided to leave Hungary as a family group, mainly to help their twins. The parent's names were Eva and Tibor Varga and they were hoping to eventually get to the USA. Their group was made up of parents in their late thirties, a girl about eight and the boy six. The twins were about four or five. I even remember the name of the twins which was Peter and Paul (not too difficult to remember, even for me).

The boredom in the camp was acute, mainly during the long, dark, wet, cold evenings in spite of the weekly dance. Later a weekly film show would happen and using the Camp Commander's private cinema equipment and films.

I noticed a small group of fellows, bored inmates in the hut next door and I remember one of them had a badly deformed leg. It looked like it had been broken but was not set properly when healing. Later on, I found out that it had been broken deliberately during an interrogation, then he was thrown back into his cell and it just healed wrongly with no medical assistance. It happened at No. 60 Andrassi Utca (street), Budapest - the most feared and hated address in the country. It was the AVO (Hungarian Secret Police headquarters) with a long pedigree. It was firstly the German Gestapo HQ, then the Russian KGB and then the AVO had been there. In 2002, it opened as a black museum called The Terror House and I went in there with the boys on one of our visits with some apprehension and recognised lots of our history but not showing any details of the torture chambers which was well below ground level, thus completely soundproof from outside. It shook me up quite a bit; much more than I had anticipated and I needed a stiff drink or two immediately afterwards.

If my memory serves me right, they had a pulley with handcuffs on the end where a poor soul was pulled off his feet by one or two hands, or one or two legs, just above a drainage hole in the floor. In the corner was some crude electrical connection and a high pressure, neatly coiled hosepipe.

The place was so secretive in nature that nobody knew much about it until about 2000, when the first journalists were allowed in, so the rumours and speculation were rife until then. One of the main questions was, "How did the AVO manage to get rid of all the bodies?" There were only two or three people out of every ten, who managed to walk out. The rumours included giant mincing machines grinding the bodies down, minus the skulls and were then flushed down the main sewer into the Danube for fish and crab food. Fishermen would find the odd hand or foot caught up in their nets. The cell floors were angled towards a drainage hole that went straight into the Danube.

The other theory was that the bodies were dissolved in a large acid bath. One thing that did get recorded was that ambulances were regularly called to remove bodies and broken dying men and thus, the responsibility was placed on traffic accidents and other incidents. More than half of the wardens were middle-aged women who apparently enjoyed inflicting mind-boggling pain on people and were very good at refining these techniques, mainly wiring up people and introducing unbelievable pains through the penis or wiring up female prisoner's nipples and vaginas. They sometime used a clip to wire the poor wretches' tongues. There were studies that showed that anyone who spent more than three month's time there and somehow managed to survive, definitely needed an 'emotional Zimmer frame' to be able to function as near normal.

Even thinking back about those stories makes me feel quite queasy especially the various techniques used, such as sleep deprivation, constant verbal abuse, one meal a day with a tiny, galvanised tray pushed under the door. If the occupants were too slow or ill, the guard would give it a good kick so most of the contents would end up on the floor, with the guards laughing, "Eat off the floor, you pig". A stew was sometimes provided with no spoon to eat it, forcing people to eat like pigs. They tried to break every last spark of defiance lurking in each person - they would not know if it was daytime or night and as this all happened underground and with manipulated light routines, you were not even able to count the days you spent in there. They would also vary the mealtimes too for additional disorientation purposes. They recorded the sound of torture when people would plead for their lives and confessed anything that did or did not happen. These recordings were broadcast through the intercom for hours and hours on end at high volume. This technique was later discontinued as it also affected the guards, including those who wore some ear protectors of an early design. These things were going on for years in great secrecy and even if it had come to light, no newspaper, magazine, or radio would be daft enough to publish or broadcast the story. It would be dismissed out of hand as pure fantasy by a vicious and deranged minds in authority.

There was an incident, I cannot pinpoint the exact time, when a Czechoslovakian Prime Minister jumped out of a third-floor window in Prague as he found this a favoured option, compared to the torture he was being put under. This was reported in the papers as Gomulka (accidentally "fell out of a window and later died of his injuries"). That was the quotation; it is my recollection; I do not actually have the official version. (Having looked this up this was probably Jan Masaryk, the Czech Foreign Minister, who was reported to have died by suicide on 10 March 1948 but was this official statement was treated with a high degree of skepticism by the West).

I'm grateful I was not part of any of these dreadful stories but hearing it even second or third hand still disturbs me a half a century later. There were some statistics to show the suicide rate of the ex-inmates was more than three times the national average and those were the ones that who were actually lucky enough to get out of 60, Andrassi Utca alive!

I heard some of the notorious conditions from events at 60, Andrassi Utca, which were probably the worst, but there were several other similar places that existed throughout the country where political prisoners were kept in purpose-built wings. However, from the outside, they appeared to be ordinary, 'normal- looking' prisons.

A group of people came over to 'entertain' us in the evenings. One man who was actually held at Andrassi Utca, told us in graphic and disturbing detail about the conditions he experienced. The cells were just like a cage, about 2 metres by 1 metre (six feet by three feet) with a bare concrete floor and equipped with a straw-filled mattress and one small pillow. There was no toilet or bucket to be slopped out each morning, so the poor inhabitant had to relieve themselves on the floor and the guard would then provide water from a high-pressure hose to clean the cell and the prisoner, especially the face. It was so powerful that if you were not able to turn away, it could gouge out your eyes or at the least, severely damage them. After those regular 'cleanings', which was the only means of getting any type of wash, prisoners would try to survive sleeping on soaked mattresses.

You wore your own clothing that you had when you got brought in but, after a few months, it was more than likely torn off your body from the jets of water. The guards would then throw in some old army uniforms which the army sent to be incinerated.

I wonder how many of these poor wretches even survived more than a few weeks.

Hungary 1956, Two Worlds Apart

Chapter 11 – Making My Way In The New World

Settling in Staines

The Labour Exchange in the camp set up a job interview for me with Girlings Ferro Concrete Co. Ltd in their offices at Great Southwest Road, Feltham, Middlesex for a job as a trainee draughtsman. I managed to get there by using a bus, changing three times along the way, and using a few travel vouchers. I met a lovely of gentleman, the Chief Draftsman, Mr. Arthur Napper. We had a lively interview, making our best efforts to try and convey what we wanted to say with no Hungarian on his part and my 'wide' knowledge of English vocabulary of perhaps 200-300 words at most.

I had a very basic dictionary, cobbled together in great haste by some charity organisation, including not more than 100 or so pages. Half of these were devoted to Hungarian and the other to the English side containing only the most basic words. Interestingly enough, I'd been using this for months on end until the first and last dozen became completely tattered and unreadable. During that particular interview, Mr. Napper asked me a question by pointing to the pages in my dictionary and I tried to answer by pointing to the right word in the dictionary. This went on for a long time and then he produced his slide rule, passed it over to me and after lots of furious head nodding from me, he understood I could use and then we carried on with a formula to calculate the stress in a beam with a lot more positive head nodding. I was then offered the job as a trainee draftsman.

It carried the princely salary of £9 a week, less the deduction for Income Tax and National Insurance. I am not actually sure whether it was my potential usefulness or if it was more to 'help those poor Hungarian refugees', or possibly Mr Girling's need to find another draughtsman.

Meanwhile, the WVS (Women Voluntary Service) tried to find me a lodging nearby. They were successful as there was a small bedroom available nearby at a place called Colwall, Welley Road, Wraysbury, with the Hodgkins family for a trial period of six months. I actually stayed there near enough seven years. At the Bridge Street bus stop, a handsome, military-looking Hungarian gentleman met me with his neatly trimmed moustache on his motorbike. He took me to the Hodgkins some four or five miles away.

My motorcyclist friend was Janos (John) Kovacs who lived on the other side of the Thames in Egham with his very pretty blonde wife, Irma, and young son Wolfie (William) and I forged a life-long friendship with his family. He was a very gentile, soft spoken man, a real gentleman with two great loves, classical music (mainly opera) and his family garden. He had been a lieutenant in the Hungarian Air Force in the fighter squadron who was shot down over Austria towards the end of the war. He stayed there and met his wife Irma, who was working in the NAAFI, and eventually they got married and made their way to live in England.

When I telephoned Irma recently (early 2018), who lives in Great Malvern these days, to confirm or correct some of my facts, my ageing brain had told me a different story. I'm not sure how I got it all wrong, or if her memory was starting to play up at bit. I noticed for the first time that her hearing had also started to worsen. When I mentioned my data, she said that Janos was not shot down over Austria as I thought at all but over Hungary. She also said she had never worked in the NAAFI with some other confusing explanation I could not follow. She said they met at a tea-dance when Janos was in full and rather dashing uniform. She said that he was the most dashing and handsome man in the dance hall. She also said they did not get married because of some regulation prohibiting the marriage but I could not get the information about where and when they actually got hitched.

I did not get any explanation why England was the destination for them but finally found out why they went to Brentford as there were lots of vacancies in the cotton and textile industries. They worked there for some time and through personal contacts between their Hungarian compatriots, found vacancies in Slough. Janos was a very highly experienced, technical man and he managed to get a job immediately with Black and Decker in their main factory on the Bath Road, in Colnbrook - just the other side of London Heathrow airport where he actually worked for about forty years until his retirement.

Apparently, he was promoted several times and had an invention which, when applied to the process they worked on, reduced the time of production by nearly half and saving considerable amounts of time and money. I believe they received a very handsome bonus for this. Before he retired, he was made the Department Head of the overall works control for the whole of Black and Decker.

Before ending the Kovacs part of the story, I must point out that Irma was an excellent cook and able to produce these mouth-watering dishes of food like Viennese Schnitzel. Around Christmas time, she would also make the traditional Austrian apple strudel, spiced with cinnamon and the taste would linger in your mouth for hours after. She was able to produce all this in their pokey little kitchen, but I drew up plans to extend it and was also involved in building it. After that, the old kitchen diner became one big-sized kitchen and living area and was so cosy they used it constantly as a main living area.

A helping hand

Ray and Pat Hodgkins and their young son Timothy lived in a house outside of Staines. Ray worked as a sales representative for Tootals (a clothing company), although today they would probably call him a Sales Executive. Pat, who preferred to be called Patricia, worked in the same place as a fashion model until she got married, then gave up the work. Ray was a very clever man with a wide knowledge of virtually everything with a degree MA (Oxford) with his English, French and history degrees. He was also a very good looking, tall man. Pat was also a rather 'dishy' looking woman with just a hint of a Harrogate accent (not that I could detect it with my pigmy-sized English knowledge). Ray used to say, "my head is crammed full of useless information". I totally disagree as he had excellent general knowledge.

Ray was a bit of a philanthropist who tried to help anyone who needed help. In other words, lame ducks like me and one night he turned up in the evening with a Chinese or Korean girl who had been mugged and was lost in London with nowhere to stay. He and Pat put her up for the night and the next morning he took her back to London.

The Hodgkins originally offered their small spare bedroom to another Hungarian refugee, a woman with a young son. The WVS came over with a counteroffer of a 23-year-old young man with no children as the Hodgkins were hoping to find someone with a young boy as company for their own son Tim.

I actually settled into 'poly-strange' or 'Oxford syndrome', where everything was strange. The language, the people, their customs and habits, food, workplace, money (which was most confusing as I'd grown up in metric world, so pence, shillings, pounds, and guineas added to the chaos and added further confusion. Why did the pound sign a capital L and the Pence a lower-case D? (I suspected it was introduced to confuse foreigners!) Why the strange, semi-slang names of tuppences, thruppence, bob and higher up ponies, and monkeys.

I got the bus from home to Staines Bridge Street for approximately 10-15 minutes ride and then to another bus which took passengers to Hatton Cross bus stop. Another five minutes' walk to the firm on the Great Western Road, one of the main arterial routes towards Hounslow in London. The firm had quite a large premises and was on the opposite side of the road to the giant BOAC (British Overseas Airways Corporation) hangar, close to Heathrow airport.

A draftsman in England

Girlings manufactured all types of prefabricated concrete structures, mainly support beams and lintels but also re-structured stone exterior cladding panels which were used in the industrial or multi-storey buildings. Industrialised or semi-industrialised construction were buzz words of the time and we competed against our major rival, Bison's, who were based just round the corner from us.

Casting of all the structural beams, which was the firm's main bread and butter, was cast outdoors in all weathers. Thus, it needed a lot of land for this operation. The firm also had two other factories, one in Kirkintilloch and one in Glasgow.

Our very long, prefabricated drawing office was all homemade, with the supporting pairs of columns at about 12 foot in the centre and intermediate purlins, forming a central aisle. At each side, there were seven or eight large, homemade desks with a large top, a small drawer for our own drawing equipment nearer to us and a smaller one at the end for personal use like daily papers, packed lunches and gloves or scarves in the winter.

On the other side of the aisle was the most senior draftsman, Claude Sutton. His wife worked in the office on the opposite side of the road at the giant BOAC factory. She was very kind and tried to help by giving me lifts to Staines when my motorbike had problems, or the car broke down.

When they prepared lunch, they would sometimes make pies to feed 'those poor starving refugees. Behind Mr.

Sutton, was David Flaherty, then Ron Knight, plus two extra people who would vary from time to time and at the very end was the printing room where all the drawings were copied (I don't remember the process they followed or what it was called). Copies were taken 10 or more times as required. They were trimmed and folded carefully for the post van to collect every evening. Usually, a retired gentleman was employed for this part time work and his duties included dispensing the tea at exactly and 10 and 4'o clock from an uninsulated urn and to wash up after. Cups had so many chips and missing parts that you could hardly see the edges, as the firm only replaced broken ones – a missing handle or two did not warrant this extravagant expenditure! Sometimes there were 'ACCIDENTAL' breakages. I wonder why the worst hand-less cups had this fate!

From the other side of the office was Mr. Napper's office (the chief draftsman), with a glass-enclosed office and drawing board as he sometimes had to muck in if pressure of the work was drowning us. There was a time when we had to take short cuts as we did not have adequate time, so somebody produced a large sheet with 'we do not have the time do the work properly but have plenty of time to do it twice'. It was put up one evening but by the morning, it had somehow got torn down and then a second copy then emerged the following morning to the annoyance of the management. When I started, I was put on the end of Mr. Napper's office as I needed the most help but later, moved behind Claude Sutton as we worked together with structural calculations.

The building was a standard design with a long continuous strip light centrally and angled-poised lights over our drawing boards. Light was essential for our work. In the wars, there was no insulation at all. The roof was a single skin, uninsulated asbestos sheets and the Crittals steel windows ran the full length of both sides of the building at desk level. Of course, at the time, it was single glazed.

The heating was good as one could not use gloved hands to do delicate, finickity, complicated work. A four-inch diameter cast iron pipe ran the full length of the building on both sides at skirting level (even though there was no skirting) and was fed by the rear boiler from the rear entrance by the WC and cloakroom. The building was also intended to provide offices for our four estimators and carried on further to home the despatch office, home to drivers, crew, loaders, and lorries as well the mobile cranes.

An interesting point was the works Foreman, called Harry, who was very short, maybe four feet nine inches, five feet at most. He had a very good pedigree as he was a Commando in the Second World War and went to France as an SAS officer behind enemy lines to carry out raids. I believe it was to blow up some harbour installation. The mission was a great success apparently. In spite of his size, none of his gang or lorry drivers, over six feet, ever dared to argue with him. The firm also used Harry as a photographic model when taking pictures of various largish structures, as his small size emphasised the huge size of the structure, he stood next to.

We shared our drawing office with Terry somebody (forgot the name), Cyril Holland and the most senior staff were John and Tony Girlings, the two sons of the two brothers who originally started the firm in the Second World War, making the most successful Anderson (air raid) shelters.

These brothers were Marcus and Ronald Girling. Marcus being the technical man and Ron was the marketing and business guru. Ron had one son called David and Marcus had twin boys. The twins were both tall, blond, and very handsome rugby players with fast cars and dozens of girlfriends. At work, they were simply playboys. Tony was not too bad as Rep, but John was a complete waste of space. He was supposed to be the overall Works Manager but was only a figurehead as the various Foremen got on with the actual work.

It was quite interesting that John had a spare draftsman's desk, and he would pile up paperwork to the roof. Even if he sat down to try and clear the work, he'd have to clear a space to be able to begin. Someone took a photo of it and pinned it to the company drawing board, but it once again disappeared the following day.

I started to settle well, and people were very helpful but sometimes they had to have their fun. For about four or five months my colleagues did all the telephone work for me. One of our Fixer Foreman, a giant-sized Irishman actually called Paddy and an accent that I could still not understand today, phoned me with enquiries on my drawing. Nobody else would answer. I picked up the phone and tried to sort out his problem but after trying several times, raising my voice, and using the same words over and over again in the hope he would understand. (Which I believe is the standard way to overcome the language barrier).

Eventually, Mr. Napper who was trying to get his flock back to work came to my rescue. Thank goodness these situations happened less and less frequently and eventually stopped.

There was banter going on all the time in the office, trying to alleviate or reduce the monotony of the long office hours. I worked 8.30 am to 5.30 pm with an hour for lunch except on Saturdays when we finished at 12.30pm and sometimes later at 2pm. This banter included things like, "You bloody foreign Git!" When I looked up hurt, they would then point at someone else - "Not you; that Irish/Welsh person over there!"

As I spent the best part of eight years in that office, I should mention that from a confused and slightly frightened foreigner, I achieved the post of Chief Technical Designer on press stress design. I must describe the processing system as it's rather technically intriguing. The design concept uses re-enforcing rods which were put at the bottom of the concrete beam. Here, it was distributed all over the beam. We used stainless steel cables, slightly cramped for better grip which then stretched considerably and used in very high-quality concrete (i.e. – one, one and half and three wires, instead of up to four). The calculations are very complicated as each of those wires could contain between 10 and 26 in a beam and could be located anywhere depending on the required loading. If it becomes overstressed, it will take up a banana shape with an upwards camber which is unacceptable for a flat roof or floor. If there is no upward camber the beam will not carry the design load which makes it useless. To calculate the exact location of each wire, it could take at least a half hour or more. This was for one single beam on the job and there could be dozens on a single project.

I noticed after designing dozens and dozens of the beams that there was a relationship between them. When not too busy, I designed a calculator which was a little bit like a slide rule. The carpenter's shop made it for me from a good quality $1/8^{th}$ plywood. Feeding in the stress on one face, it would give the exact location on each of the wires reading from the back. This device was so successful that one hour plus of manual calculations could be reduced to ten minutes or so. The Directors were so pleased they ordered two further copies to be sent to the other branches. This device was also 100% accurate and eliminated any mistakes done using the old method.

The stressing bed, normally held of a dozen or so wires, was grouped together for mass production. Each bed was divided length wise to the correct beam length and with precisely drilled holes for the wires to pass through. When each wire is located and anchored with a self-locking wedge, they were attached to a hydraulic ram and stressed to the required lengths. Then a very high-quality concrete would fill the beds to the top of the mould, vibrated to compact it and then the top edge was finished by hand. Quick-setting concrete was used because the wires could easily be cut after three days, and the beams could be lifted in five days.

It was interesting to see that the (now closed) Tarmac concrete factory on the Chichester Bypass uses exactly the same system today, except the casting was done inside a long building and the vibrators were built in with underfloor heating to reduce the curing time.

Once everything was ready by using a large lorry jack to pump it through, a second man called a Stressor would join as the pumping got too hard for one man. After thirty minutes, the men had to call it a day, for a well-earned cuppa and left the concrete to get on with its setting. Seeing this struggle twice a week just outside the office window, I went to see John Girlings who was supposed to be the Work Manager to try and persuade him to buy an electric ram. Of course, as expected, the answer was, "We can't afford that sort of money". I argued without success. The next slack time in the office, I got down to calculate the actual cost of the ram, installation and delivery was some £300 against the cost of man hours. With the total cost of holiday and sick pay it became clear that the total cost could be recuperated in six stressing. (i.e., just under 4 months). The ram was on order within 48 hours and happily arrived a few weeks later.

The Drawing Office was entirely male dominated with no females in sight. Not that there were many in the firm anyhow. There was Jean, a rather overweight woman, a Miss Winterbourne, a telephonist/receptionist, not that we hardly got any visitors. To me she was a typical spinster, thin as a rake and of questionable age with thin-wired rim glasses, double string pearl necklace and never a hint of a smile and rather unfriendly. She had groomed hair behind her ears and constantly battled with white hairs that showed through from her dark hair dye. The whites were definitely winning the battle! All those culminated on the top of her head in a neat bun which I never understood how it was kept at the top without any obvious fixings. She was all the time dressed in a beautifully starched and ironed white blouse and a long purplish skirt. She was the general

Secretary to Ron Girling. The other secretary was Mrs Sylvia Baker, who was extremely good-looking, young, and slim and a few years older than me. She used to come to work on the bus but Bernard, her husband, picked her up after work each day. After a few years, they got her an Austin Mini Minor. Bernard was working nearby, I think, in Hounslow as a Chief Cashier for Barclays Bank. Sylvia was also the secretary to Mr. Fielder who was the firm's General Manager.

One day she asked me to come to their house for Sunday afternoon tea. While in their house, we struck up a deep and lasting friendship and I discovered that Bernard was very interested in photography, and we enrolled together to a local Polytechnic photography course. The course provided a room with podium and lots of spotlights, backgrounds, other lighting equipment tripods and photographic models. Sometimes the model would be an adult woman in some sort of swimsuit or bikini but mostly it would be young girls borrowed from the local dance school. We also had expert tuition on how to arrange the lighting to the best effect, highlighting, masking etc. and we also had to develop the film and enlarge it. I bought all the chemicals required for the different processes, including the trays and darkroom lighting. I commandeered our cloak room in the White Lodge for this work. A rather complicated but quite satisfactory type of work, but I could not continue to work on colour processing as it was beyond my capabilities.

Bernard and I started a friendly competition between each other as to who would be able to create the best piece of work.

While I was sitting with them for Sunday tea, Bernard produced a family photo album, which is the standard first aid to start conversation flowing. In the album was a photograph of Sylvia in a swim suit in a beauty competition some years earlier. Obviously, she did not like to show this around, but Bernard was rather proud of his lovely wife. I would then start to teach them Canasta, a long and complicated card game similar to Gin Rummy, but infinitely more complex and interesting in my opinion. It is also rather addictive.

I got hooked on this game while at university and sometimes spent half the night playing it and often all weekend. Bernard and Sylvia also got hooked on this too and made similar and regular events at the weekend meeting which also included Penny (Bernard's younger sister) who was also pretty, but so slim a strong wind would have knocked her off her feet! Sometimes we had a little party or outings with Bernard, Sylvia, Penny and Penny's spectacled boyfriend. They took me to Hampton Court palace and sometimes Bernard and I would use our time there to do some photography work of the palace and deer park. Bernard nearly had an accident there by going too near a Stag for a close-up shot and he was comically chased off out of the area. For some reason, both Sylvia and Penny were camera-shy, but I still managed to take a few sneaky ones of them which Bernard congratulated me on this major achievement.

At Girlings there was a traditional, yearly staff outing in a hired small coach down to Brighton at the weekend. The firm could not afford a day off paid work for everyone. Perhaps they were just skinflints. We did a gigantic pub crawl and finished off with a fish and chip dinner paid for by the Directors which also included a crate of beer for the homeward journey.

In one of the pubs in Brighton, above a counter, I saw some Jellied Eels for sale. In Hungary, we have a similar thing called 'Kucsonnya', which was a tasty pork product. Due to my very limited English, I didn't know what I was ordering, but ate it and actually quite enjoyed it. My colleagues explained to me what was in it by demonstrating graphically with their hands, wiggling motions of the eels. Now I knew what it was, I suddenly didn't feel so good for the journey home!

While I was still at Girlings there was an episode at work worth mentioning. This is a story which is similar to the hydraulic pump and the short sightedness of the so-called businessman in 1958. That year, Southern England experienced a rather unusual 'Big Freeze'. I remember Ray put on his car one of those cylindrical portable paraffin heaters for half an hour in the front seat, whilst having his breakfast, to warm the cabin up enough to get him to London before it froze over again. At the time, built-in car heaters were not in existence. I wonder what Health and Safety would say these days about burning paraffin heaters on the front seat of a fuel-loaded, unattended car whilst having your cornflakes and then getting into a monoxide-filled area for a 40-minute drive without the windows open.

The water pipe at the office became frozen solid under the main driveway to the works, which ruptured an old and rusty iron pipe which was only a few inches below the surface. Three or four men were detailed to dig up and repair the pipe. Kango hammers opened up a trench and the men were instructed to put the new pipe into the correct depth. As I watched them do this from my office window, who was about 20 to 30 feet away, there was a let-up in the freeze at one point, and everything began to thaw out. The men were instructed to fill up the trench and put the water pipes back where they were before as they didn't want to lose another day of production. This freeze also caused havoc on the general roads and apart from the usual limbs being broken from people falling over on untreated roads and pavements, there were many vehicle collisions and daily scrapes. One day I was going to work, waiting in a car at the traffic light and the turning to Feltham. The camber of the road was rather severe and the car in front of me started to slide on the camber towards the left and it just touched the fully loaded milk float which caused the float to move and hit the curb, at which time the entire contents of the float tipped everywhere all over the road with the sound of tingling glass everywhere.

Ray once suggested that I should go and get some 'real' shopping experience. As of now, I only had bought cigarettes, matches and postage stamps. Even those were purchased at the Sunnymead stores where I knew Avril, who ran the shop. At the time, I needed toothpaste, so I set out for Staines on the bus. On the journey, I carefully rehearsed what I was going to say in my head as I did not wish to make a pig's ear of my sentence.

I went into Boots on the High Street in Staines and went up to a rather pretty young girl about the same age as me and said in my very best, compound fractured English, "Can I have some Tit-Paste please?"

The girl could obviously not understand me, and I tried to repeat it. Even then, half of the shop had started to look at us. I eventually pointed to the item with my finger as I'd used that brand before and was then able to buy it and managed to quickly escape from the shop.

When I arrived home, I told Ray and Pat what had happened. To the endless merriment of Ray, putting on my continental accent and repeating my mistake many, many times.

While in Wraysbury with the Hodgkins, I had a lot of trouble with my teeth. I had to go to the dentist, which luckily enough lived 150 yards away in a large bungalow at the junction of Valley Road and The Avenue where he also had his dental surgery. His dental nurse was 'home grown', also known as his wife. I had gum disease (advanced periodontitis). I am ashamed to say that in my early life, I had appalling dental hygiene as by the age of 28 I had to have a small plate in my mouth. I hope that the next generation in Hungary will have much better and healthier teeth. In England, every household with children would receive a war cry after food or before bedtime, "Go and brush your teeth!". In my childhood I never heard that sentence ever addressed to me. I naturally had my own toothbrush and paste, but we only brushed our teeth before visiting the dentist and you would only go to see the dentist if you had toothache. This would normally end with a filling or extraction. We did not have check-ups and regular cleaning was not part of our vocabulary or routine.

Ray and I did a lot of work together on his garden as I was at a loose end and was glad to do something which was also a lot of fun. Opposite the Hodgkin's bungalow were several interlocking, now redundant, gravel pits and only the village end of these pits were still working. These pits would fill up from rain and ground water naturally and were crystal clear as they had no time to silt up. It was possible to see the very bottom of these lakes some twenty or thirty feet down. On the summer weekends, when sunny, we would climb over the wire fence and have picnics to the delight of Tim. Often someone called Trixie would join us when she came down for some weekends and she even came swimming with us in the lake.

Ray was a real 'twitcher'. Anything he did not know about British birds was not worth knowing. He did, however, confess he lacked such knowledge in sea birds. He wrote several articles on birds, most of which were published, not just in the RSPB magazines but other publications as well. He was one of the officials of the RSPB, but I do not know any more than that. One warm summer weekend morning, it was arranged to get up at 4.30am as Ray had heard that part of the dawn chorus was from the singing of a nightingale, a little bit further down the lane in a thicket somewhere. We were rewarded for our early rising efforts, with some amazing singing from the bird and I've never heard anything so exquisite and haunting before or ever since.

Sometimes we would go over to the acres of gravelled area to find birds eggs with the help of Ray. We would find plovers and peewits who hide their eggs in the pebbles for camouflage and they could only be found if you quietly observed where the birds would fly back to in order to feed their chicks. There were willow warblers, wagtails, and reed warblers too.

Ray was a very keen fisherman, and I went with the family down some lovely rivers around the Oxford area where he would try his hand at fly-fishing although not very successfully. He also tried eel fishing. One summer evening, near dusk, Ray's best friend from work, Ralf Turner, came and organised a night fishing session. They geared up with half a dozen rods, reels, nets, and other fishing paraphernalia including a dozen or so beers. I accompanied them although my total fishing pedigree in Hungary was one edible-sized fish which I caught on my homemade bamboo rod, a few metres of fishing line, float, hooks, lead weight and all of it cobbled together by me. We marched down to Miss Young's landing stage with her permission of course and we started to fish.

I tried my hand at it but Ray had to bait my hooks and then after that I settled down to wait. I had the first bite, but in my anxiety, I was too quick and rough to haul it out and I lost the eel. Ray managed to get one and then, to my delight, I got one myself, then another. Eventually we packed it in as we'd run out of beer, and it was close to midnight and getting very cold. Next morning Ray cleaned the eels and gutted them, filleted, and battered them into a frying pan. The muscles reacted to the hot fat and started to move in the pan. Pat refused to touch it after that, so Ray had to cook and when I got to eat it, they were delicious.

While with the Hodgkin's, I had time to contact the International Red Cross making enquiries about Zoltan's whereabouts because I did not wish to lose touch with him if I could help it. The Red Cross could not locate him because I was not sure what his final destination had been.

At Wraysbury, I kept corresponding with Marika (my fiancé back in Hungary) and we wrote most weeks, later fortnightly and then slowly less and less. We both realised that our situation was hopeless as I could and would not, go back to Hungary and the Hungarian government would not let her leave. I was psyching myself up to write one of those 'Dear John' letters when she beat me to the punch and wrote me 'THAT' letter, breaking up our engagement and announcing that she had become engaged to a lecturer at her university. In many ways it was a relief and so much had happened since we last saw each other our relationship had cooled down and it didn't hurt too much.

I bought a 500 cc Triumph motorbike for a princely sum of £60. Everything was OK with it mechanically for a few months, but I found that it was definitely too heavy to handle and a bit much for me. At the same time, it was lovely not to have to queue at bus stops, waiting in the pouring rain or snow. One winter morning, whilst riding to work, I tested the road condition to see if it was ice-free, but before I got my answer, I was overtaken by a very large gravel lorry, fully loaded with freshly excavated gravel with the ground water still pouring out of the bottom. As the water was hitting the road and freezing on contact it became an ice rink. When I hit this patch of black ice, which I hadn't seen, the bike went out from under me, and I found myself sliding on the road very fast on my elbows and knees accompanied by a terrifying screech of the lorry brakes. My instinct told me to carry on clinging onto the bike to give the lorry driver a chance to be able to avoid me.

Eventually it went quiet, and the driver got out of his cabin and came over to see whether I was OK or not. After reassuring him that I was OK, I got on my bike and went to work. The only damage was the lack of skin on my elbow, one knee and base of my chest caused by the slide and the bike headlight glass was broken and the petrol tank got a dent. Coming home that same evening, I found that the lorry was still fully loaded and sunk down under the weight of the gravel, axle deep, where the driver had to steer to avoid me. The lorry had to be offloaded before they could pull it off to the side of the road. After that, Ray insisted that the motorbike was advertised for sale if I wanted to stay living with them.

By this time, I had got used to my freedom to travel and decided to buy my first little car. I found a three-year-old, four-door Austin A30 and bought it for £325. At the time, the second-hand car market wasn't very good for the buyer, and you'd be lucky to knock off £5 from the asking price. The actual forecourt price was £350, and I got a reduction as I paid in cash.

I was virtually a daily visitor to other people like Bob and Nellie Chilton. They liked my company (I don't know why) and we enjoyed my English lessons including asking me for Hungarian words like 'Bisztos' ('Sure') and a lot of S.S.S from both of them. In Hungarian, plurals always end differently, and I never got it that the end of the S made a plural. We played tongue twisters in both languages as it helped articulation using English or Hungarian like:

Peter Piper picked a peck of pickled peppers.

How many pecks of pickled peppers did Peter Piper pick?

If Peter Piper picked a peck of pickled peppers, Where's the peck of pickle peppers Peter Piper picked?
Six shiny seashells lay shimmering on the shore
Csendes csiga csinositgat kicsi csodas hazacskajan
Peckes cickany-ficko picike kocka-vacka

On some hot summer weekends, I quite often walked up to the Chiltons for a refreshing swim in the river (Thames). While doing that from a landing stage I made myself useful by pulling up lorry loads of weeds from the riverbed at low tide as the river at Wraysbury is tidal and at low tide it was only chest deep. The seaweed seemed to choke the river and I tried to clear it as much as I could. Bob had a little rowing boat and he used to row over the other side of the river (the deeper part) to do some fishing in the evenings.

My river weeding work was essential so that the propellers of the boats would not choke if there were too many. Bob and Nellie had a good next-door neighbour, Victor Palmer, if my memory is correct. He owned an up-market wallpaper business which included a range of real silk-covered paper. He owned a motorboat moored on the same landing stage as Bob's and he allowed Bob to borrow it whenever he wanted. He did these two or three times a year in the summer and we made a little party of us to go up river to Marlow and one year we actually took part in the yearly Henley Regatta. Victor was a bachelor and only came down once or twice a year for a week or occasional weekend and Bob was looking after his launch and made sure it had enough mooring rope at low tide and pulled out of the water at high tide when the river was flooding.

Ray and Pat had two or three ducks in their chicken run. In spite of Ray's advice, Pat gave them all names and she also gave them edible kitchen waste. She became quite fond of them. When they had stopped laying, the idea was to prepare them for the table, but Pat refused point blank, so they were taken to the river (Thames) and were let free instead. Ray and Pat went down to the river daily with some food for a few days but after a while they were lost in amongst all the other wildfowl on the water.

Moving on

Pat had another baby during this time and my bedroom became baby Adams' room. Ray and I did a lot of work to the extension they had planned which was supposed to be my new, luxury bedroom with en-suite toilet and shower. We dug and concreted all the footings and flooring. I only lived in this luxurious surrounding for six months, but then I was told I needed to find a new place to live as they'd decided to give up the work at Tootals, as Ray found the morning journey was a nightmare trying to get in and out of London. It made him very miserable and short-tempered.

They moved to Oxford, where Ray and Pat were to start a travel agency and aptly would call it 'Town and Gown', referring to the business generated in the 'town' of Oxford, and the 'gown' of the university where a very large volume of business was generated from lecturers and students. They bought a large shop in Summer Town (a suburb of Oxford) which they would turn into a travel agency. It had two upper floors for the offices and a small flat in the attic. I believe that purchase and refurbishment was with Trixie's money as I knew she was an integral part of the business. Ray and Pat bought a lovely home called Rose Cottage in Stadhampton, which I visited quite regularly at the weekends. Jeremy would also visit as a schoolboy often. He was Pat's nephew and Marty (her Mum) would visit one or twice a year. I didn't like her at all as I found her a manipulating and calculated kind of person. I am not surprised that her husband left her and legged it, possibly emigrated.

After the announcement that Ray and Pat were moving to Oxford, we put the local newspaper, the Bush Telegraph, to work to find a new room for me, mainly through Len and Avril at the Sunnymead store. Eventually, it produced one result in Ousley Road, a room owned by a widow in her middle age for ten quid a week. My room was very clean and spacious in a modern bungalow. However, after a week or so, things 'started to happen'. The first thing to occur was one evening when I arrived home from work. I found that all my cigarettes had disappeared which were in the bottom of my wardrobe. There were several hundred which I purchased from a friend shortly before who had been abroad and had brought them back as duty free. Her explanation was that they were soaked whilst washing out the bottom of my wardrobe. I was thinking about calling the police but decided against this. The washing out of the wardrobe was not necessary as her furniture was practically new.

The second incident happened when I next went shopping. We had a 'robbery' and, when I called the police, the sergeant responded that this was an internal job. My weekly wage which was stored in the bedside cabinet was taken. The police noticed that the window had been smashed from the inside and found a hammer hidden (badly) under the landlady's bed with some glass fragments still on the hammer head. I was asked if I wanted to press charges. After a long deliberation, I decided against this as the police file contained several previous charges for her on this. Also, she was drunk and disorderly twice, which was dealt with by a previous warning and Grievous Bodily Harm against her ex-husband and other things. I was asked again, knowing this now and if she was charged, she would have definitely gone to jail. The police and I decided that if she re-reimbursed me for my loss, it would keep a drunken old lady out of prison.

Her culinary skill was strictly tied to the frying pan. She was supposed to provide 'half-board', but 'full-board' at the weekend. Our diet was fried spam, bacon, egg, sausage, occasionally fried rice, bakes beans and fried eggs with an apple at the end of each meal. Once in a while we'd get some fish fingers for variety.

I was sick to death of the place - the burglaries, terrible food and fake fish fingers had brought me to the last straw and this straw came on one Sunday afternoon when I brought home a very pretty girlfriend who I'd met the night before at a dance. If I remember correctly, I went home to get my camera as we'd planned to go to the 'punchbowl' (a beauty spot) in Windsor Great Park where all inward facing sides would be home to many amazing Azalea bushes. It was a scorching hot day, similar to that which we experienced recently in the UK (2018). My landlady was coming toward us down the corridor stark naked except distinctly blue knickers that I will never forget. I have to tell you it was not a pleasant sight. An old woman with all the flabs and folds hanging around. She saw us coming in her direction and as we met, she was obviously, hugely embarrassed and retreated to her room and we did the same, mentally scarred for life. I wonder why my new, lovely girlfriend was never keen to ever see me again after that sight.

We had a visit the following weekend from the landlady's son, a very nice, middle-aged gentleman. In conversation, I learnt that he was the Managing Director of a rather large firm in the city (I have forgotten the firm's name). He thanked me for not sending his drunken mother to jail as after three previous convictions and this situation, she would have been locked up. I immediately gave my notice to leave and started to look for new digs frantically. They were not very easily available, but I managed to find one in Staines by looking in the classifieds, shop windows and word of mouth which I found by accident. This was equally poor, and the 'food' was terrible.

The next one was Hightend. They gave me notice after a week or so of staying there as a relative was coming back from abroad and they needed the room.

The next one (by then I was in desperation) was OK, but the area was the roughest part of Staines so I could never sleep properly in case I would find my A30 Austin on bricks and the four wheels gone the following morning.

In the village of Wraysbury, I lived in Valley Road. I met a young chap, about my age called Peter Johnson, who was working at the local plant nursery. Every lunchtime, he popped in 'The George' (his usual watering hole) for a quick pint and a sandwich or pork pie. The pub was a real 'local', very popular and friendly. It had a very large room at the back, which was let out by Fred Pike, the Landlord, for various events such as village meetings, wedding receptions and such like. The landlord was a very passionate boxing fan and he let it out to his hero, the then British heavyweight boxing champion, Henry Cooper, and entourage who once fought the world champion Cassius Clay who later, after converting to Islam, changed his name to Muhammad Ali. Bob and Nelly Chilton were also devoted boxing fans and would not miss a fight shown on the television. During my boring evenings, I would join them and got quite hooked on this sport.

Peter and I, while watching Henry Cooper sparring with his twin brother George with a pint in our hands, started to talk to one another. We discovered we both lived on the same road, just opposite sides and ends.

At the time I was a very sober young man and Peter and I made regular dates to watch the boxing and I got very fond of English beer. We soon formed a long and lasting friendship, and, amid my desperate and miserable existence, he told me that he found a detached house to rent from an old primary school friend (Babs). She was the daughter of the Staines main car dealer who had a large showroom opposite Thames Bridge. Her Grandma left her the house as in inheritance, but she didn't want to live in it. Therefore, she was letting it out fully furnished.

Peter invited me to join him as he was not happy at home sharing his place with a complete stranger. I was very glad for this offer and didn't hesitate to accept even though I hadn't even seen the place. "YES PLEASE!!"

We prepared to move into 'The White Lodge', Pulley, Green Road, Egham, Surrey.

Chapter 12 – White Lodge

The White Lodge was in Pooley Green Road, Egham Surrey. It was a detached, two story, flat roofed property although I believe the new owners have now added a pitched roof. It was by the Pooley Green railway level crossing on the line which runs between Staines and Egham stations. The rail line went to London Waterloo station.

Peter and I happily moved into this three-bedroom house which had a large sitting room, good sized dining room/kitchen and separate WC. The house was in a reasonable order, except for the carpet in the sitting room which has seen better days. The rest of the floors in the house were covered with linoleum.

Peter chose the bedroom opposite the bathroom and the furthest away from the noisy railway line. I volunteered for the noisiest room but had a lovely large picture window to the front looking over a small coppice and the parking places for about eight to ten cars including my Austin A30 (we have a photo of him with this car). A friend of Peter's, a chap called Dr John Webber came to share the house. I cannot recollect at which point John joined us but he was there to share the cost. I never knew how Peter knew him but he was an industrial chemist working for ICI Company as a specialist in paint technology. His offices were about half a mile down the road. He was a real loner and I believe was a year or so older than us.

We spent (or rather misspent) our happy bachelor days in the house. Peter was still going daily to his horticultural nursery where he was employed. I was still working for Messer's Girling, commuting there each day in my little Austin 30 which took me about 25-30 minutes each morning and slightly longer on the way home. Peter was working a five and a half days week and he was already showing early sign of an entrepreneurial spirit. He bought home from his firm boxes and boxes of bedding plants, pretty much as many as he could cram into his car at a knockdown price. Saturday morning would come, and John and I were just turning in bed for an extra snooze, but Peter would go instead to Staines market to sell his goods.

This blissful extra half an hour's morning sleep didn't last too much longer as I started evening classes, twice a week from 6 to 9pm at the Slough technical college which is now the University of Surrey. When I successfully completed my ONC (ordinary national certificate) I then enrolled for the next exam which was the Higher national certificate (HNC) which I never actually finished to my regret as my interest and attention was re-directed towards my future wife, Anne.

As I mentioned, Peter had good business aptitude, he did both markets at Windsor and Staines and also kept the grass immaculate at our local pub, the George, our closest watering hole, and he also worked at another pub called The Feathers. When he started, he was doing it just for beer money but later on for more serious cash on a yearly contract basis planting out all the gardens, looking after hedges and general landscaping / patios/ BBQ islands/ gazeebo's etc. He would also do some pub jobs in Wraysbury, I forget the name, but I know it has unfortunately shut down like so many pubs.

At the White Lodge, Peter and I were busy as we were unable to park outside the house due to the railway gates opening and shutting and also there was a ditch which ran parallel in front of the house and the only access was a pathway leading to the front door. We built a bridge over this ditch, Peter bought 3 telegraph poles (old but still serviceable) and we laid them side by side to make a good enough bridge, wide enough for a car but not to get in or out of it unless you were completely sober. At that time there was no drink driving laws of course. The lack of handrails didn't help and our bridge sloped a lot from the road so slippery mornings, with moss covered timber or maybe ice or snow, was always a hazard. There was no way to the bridge that could take all three of our cars. I elected to park my Austin in the coppice opposite and John decided to park further down the road.

One frosty winter morning, I went out to start the car to warm it up while I grabbed some breakfast. Unfortunately, I wasn't quite awake yet and I managed to lock the car with the engine running and with keys in the ignition which included my house keys. I was just about to force my quarter light to get in when I suddenly heard a voice "'ello, 'ello 'ello". When I explained to the police officer what I was trying to do he tried to help me fix it as it wasn't a safe situation.

We were also doing other jobs at the White Lodge, but John had a bad back 'allegedly' which meant he wouldn't offer to help with anything (a lazy bugger). We cleared the overgrown back garden using Peter's machinery as well as getting some planking and repairing the dilapidated fence between us and the neighbours, Mr and Mrs Pink's, property. They had a son too, Colin, about our age who was an extremely shy and lonely sort of chap. We would invite him to our various parties, but he'd never accept. At least, though, they couldn't complain about noises or loud music.

On Saturday nights, Peter and I would usually go to some party, local dance, or the cinema. Mostly we went to the dance at the Castle Ballrooms in Richmond every Saturday the biggest venue in southeast London except Alexander Palace, affectionately known as Ally Pally. The name of Castle Ballrooms always puzzled me as there is no castle at Richmond. There were two giant ballrooms, end to end with a large stage with a removable partition if needed. The ballrooms had beautifully sprung floors with a parquet surface and had fantastic acoustics. Every Saturday night, two full thirty-piece brass bands would play and provide the music with singers from 7pm to midnight where, with the very very strict laws at midnight everything had to stop on the sound of the national anthem.

I would not be surprised that in southeast London or Middlesex, 50% of the young generation would have all met at the Castle Ballrooms in Richmond it was so popular at the time.

In the middle of an evening there would be a half hour break from the music. Not wanting to deprive the punters of their dance, a member of the orchestra would continue to play alone so you could continue dancing. We met a lot of girls there which we would end up taking home after these nights. However, relationships lasted only a few days or months. I dated many girls over this time with no ties and nothing to worry about. I particularly remember one girlfriend called Sylvia with Jet black hair who lived in High

Road, Chiswick and I was fascinated in her family, but maybe not her quite so much. Her father was Portuguese, her mother English, her grandmother was Indian (hence the jet-black hair) and the whole family were closely tied to the English diplomatic services.

Another girl I dated I recall was Evelyn. She was working in the city for a firm making documentary films for the MOD. She was doing some editing I believe and as it was customary at her company, the employees were allowed to view the completed films. When the next film was shown she was refused entry to view this feature and when she asked why she was told that she could not view it because she was dating a foreigner (me of course) who had come from behind the iron curtain. I actually only took her out five or six times.

While living at The White Lodge Peter and I took some holidays abroad. We belonged to the Dachet Young Conservatives, not that either of us had any political views but every fortnight they provided table tennis facilities, organised trips away and abroad for long weekends. One year we flew to Paris to the Le Bourget airport and stayed at a rather dingy hotel near the Gare Du Nord railway station.

The following year we went for another long weekend to Amsterdam where I was surprised, they provided cheese with toast for breakfast which I'd never had before. We loved the numerous old picture galleries and looking at the old masters. Peter and I also went for a week to Spain on a different trip to Portbou which is a frontier town between France and Spain, and we walked through to France for a drink on a precarious cliff edge walk but we had to be careful to go back in daylight as the sheer edge on one side would drop you straight into the sea if you put a foot wrong.

While at The White Lodge I often visited Janos and Irma's as it was only a twenty-minute walk from our place in Egham. Whilst there, Irma showed her usual Austrian hospitality with lovely cakes etc. and a good chat. These visits however came with a problem, a language problem. Janos, Irma and William could all speak German which I couldn't speak, and Janos and I could speak Hungarian which Irma and William could not speak. In the end Janos put his foot down with the fantastic suggestion that from then on, we should all only talk in English.

One Saturday night, Peter got an invite from somebody, perhaps a friend of a friend, for a little bottle party which was fashionable at the time. Bring a bottle, bring a friend. The party was in a little flat near Addleston, Chertsey and Anne were there with her boyfriend at the time, some Scandinavian, possibly Swedish man. I finished up with Anne's friend who was a rather skitty, blond bombshell with masses of curly hair and we dated each other for a few weeks. After we broke up Peter then stepped in and took her out for a month or so.

I cannot recollect if Peter had always had a short beard but for some reason, I decided to grow one influenced by a current girlfriend and after a month's growth, some type of beard had grown on my face, approved by my friends, including the Hodgkin's saying "it suited me and made me look distinguished". The current girlfriend I had also thought it was rather sexy. It made my chin very itchy though and I never stopped scratching until about six months later when I'd eventually had enough and became clean shaven again.

Whilst still living at The White Lodge, Anne and I got engaged. Peter also got engaged to Jean. Whilst we were in that state, we booked a fortnight's holiday to the Mediterranean, called Lido Di Jesolo, Italy (a beach province of Venice). Everyone was going there at the time, and it was very popular. We started our journey in London and had to be at the Victoria coach terminal. From there we started a non-stop journey to our destination with a relief driver on board to take over. We only had a limited number of stops, there was a loo on board but after half an hour it began to overflow, and nobody wanted to use it. We drove all day and night right through the Pyrenees and whilst we crossed these mountains, we experienced horrendous thunderstorms and horrible hair pin bends with constant lightning showing the near abys of the road. We managed to get there for about 9pm and we had missed our evening meals. When we didn't turn up at the right time, they shut the kitchens so nobody ate anything for the entire day. We booked two double bedrooms, Jean and Anne sharing one and me with Peter. Apart from the initial journey we had a lovely holiday but dreaded our return trip to England. It turned out that the way home was uneventful with lovely sunny weather and the hair pins nowhere near as frightening and there was wonderful panoramic view of the Alps.

For both journeys there was a lot of chitter chatter and we mostly kept to ourselves which annoyed our fellow passengers. There was malicious gossip amongst the other passengers about a luggage labelling issue, but we did not put them right until the end of the trip when we arrived back to London and enjoyed ourselves seeing the red faces of the gossipers.

I was the first one to fly the nest and leave The White Lodge to get married. This was followed by Peter and then John who was the last one. John married his last girlfriend, a rather stunning looking girl, a German au pair working in the old Windsor area.

Chapter 13 - It's Been A Wonderful Life (26/11/2020)

This final chapter was written following Leo's death on 31 July 2019. Whilst writing the earlier chapters and discussing his life with family Leo often reflected that overall, he had been blessed to have had a wonderful life. This, of course, referred mainly to what he thought of as his 'safe haven' in England rather than the hardships, oppression, and injustices he had experienced in his earlier life in Hungary under two very different but equally brutal and oppressive regimes. This chapter, written after his death, outlines his 'wonderful life' in England.

Following Leo and Anne's wedding on 7TH March 1964 the happy couple initially lived in a small house in Ightham, a small rural town near Sevenoaks in Kent.

On 13 February 1965 Leo and Anne's first child was born. She was named Elizabeth Anne but has always been known as Bebba.

On 24 July 1966 their second child was born, this time a son named Nicholas Leo (Nick or Nicky to the family).

In December 1966 the young family moved from Kent to the small town of Arundel in West Sussex. At that time Arundel was a town with a population of approximately two thousand and is a picture postcard town set on two hills, the second of which is the highest and is crowned with a cathedral and a considerable castle, parts of which date back to the Norman conquest. They moved into a newly built three-bedroom house in Dalloway Road (number 16) which was located via Torton Hill which is the second, lower hill of Arundel. As they moved in just before Christmas 1966, they named the house 'Noel'. Set on the edge of Arundel this was an extremely rural beautiful location with open countryside a short walk to the south and with woodland directly to the rear of the property, accessed directly from the back gate over a little stream. This provided an idyllic English semi-rural setting to live and raise a family.

In 1967 Leo received his British naturalisation papers.

At this time Leo was working as a designer for Marley, a building company, and commuted by car daily to Robertsbridge in Kent, some fifty-three miles each way.

It wasn't too long before Leo and Anne added again to their growing family and on 12 September 1969 Joseph Adam (Joe) was born.

At some point around 1972 Leo extended the house and added a dining room at the rear with another bedroom on top.

The family enjoyed their idyllic life in Arundel and took their annual fortnight summer holidays initially in Devon in the early 1970s and then in North Wales. Leo and Anne always preferred self-catering holidays on farms which were reasonably inexpensive but again provided idyllic rural locations for the young family who always loved getting up at the crack of dawn to help out with activities such as the milking on dairy farms as well as the adventures of roaming further afield. They would often become firm friends with the owners of the farms and small holdings they stayed on. In particular there was a lovey couple called Blodwyn and David Hughes with whom they stayed on a small holding in North Wales near Caernarfon. The children loved walks in the hills with Blodwyn to pick bilberries and everyone was made to sing. Leo, being an Opera buff but having little musical talent wasn't too keen on singing.

In early 1977, much to the surprise of the three children, it was announced that Anne was again expecting. In order to cater for this addition to the family and with Leo needing a home office in mind it was decided that the family should move to a larger house. So, in November 1977, with Anne eight months pregnant, the family moved about two hundred metres down the road from Dalloway Road to the top of Torton Hill (number 40). It should be noted that Torton Hill is considered an exclusive road in Arundel to live in. A removal van was employed but there was still a fair amount of carrying possessions by hand up the road. The Torton Hill house was a much larger five-bedroom house with a large garden which, again, backed onto the same woodland as before known as Stewards Copse. Leo spent the vast majority of his spare time working in the garden which he loved. Leo developed and tended a considerable fruit and vegetable area. Producing as much home produce as possible is a very Hungarian trait. The preserving and pickling of fruit and vegetables and jams and wine making was something of a cottage industry for the household each August and September.

At the end of the garden was a sunken garden and set at the back of it was thick concrete air raid shelter built in 1940. The owners at that time must have been worried about the Luftwaffe bombers and with some justification as they would sometimes release unused bombs on their way back to the coast from London. Often, they would panic and turn back early from raids on London and, not wanting to return with bombs, they would release them if they could spot any light near the coast believing that any light was a coastal defence of some kind. The children would often come across huge craters in the nearby woodland which had by then become wooded but clearly not natural.

On 4th December 1977 the final addition to the family arrived when George Bevel was born (Bevel was Anne's father and a Cornish name).

Leo was made redundant from Marley in 1978 and set up his own business in late 1978. He had a business partner who ran operations in and around London and Leo looked after the rural areas outside London, mainly Sussex and Kent.

There was no annual family summer holiday in 1978 but in 1979 the family holiday resumed and this time a self-catering annex of a farmhouse was booked at a place called Lower Treluswell Farm, near Penryn on the outskirts of Falmouth in Cornwall. Again, this was a dairy farm and again Leo and Anne became firm friends with the tenant farmer and his wife, Mr and Mrs Champion. The family would continue to holiday at Lower Trelsuwell Farm for many years through the 1980s and early 1990s. These holidays instilled a love of Cornwall in the children that lasts to this day and passed on to grandchildren. Initially, Cornwall became a holiday destination because of the love and affinity Anne had with the county which was instilled in her as a child by her father, Bevel who was born and brought up in a house his father built in Redruth, so a proper Cornishman. As Hungary is a land locked country Leo didn't really have a healthy fear of the dangers of the sea and would often scare Anne half to death with various sea-side antics, normally involving a large inflatable dingy which was transported all over Cornwall tied to the roof-rack of the car. The dingy was once towed back by the coastguard after drifting too far into Falmouth Bay and getting into difficulty and resulted in Leo having a dressing down. Leo simply didn't understand the concept of sea currents.

Leo played badminton to a reasonable standard at Barnham St Philip Howard School on Thursday evenings and in 1980 whilst playing a match suffered a major heart attack. This was a shock to the family as Leo always appeared fit and very active. The heart attack was severe and could have been fatal but due to the fast actions of those he was playing with he thankfully survived. The heart condition was caused by a combination of hereditary issues, a poor high fat diet and smoking for twenty or so years, although he had given up smoking a few years earlier.

It was diagnosed in the early 1980s that Leo required a heart by-pass but due to lengthy waiting lists and several cancellations this did not happen until 1989. Although Leo initially took a while to fully recover, he did eventually regain his old strength and fitness. His clogged arteries in his chest had been replaced with arteries from his legs. The biggest challenge seemed to be to get back to walking properly as the leg arteries adjusted and re-developed.

Leo always took the family on holiday in England or Wales. This was not simply because of economic restrictions or the fact that foreign holidays were so much less prevalent than they are today but largely because there was an element of him being afraid to leave the 'safe haven' of the UK. In the back of his mind, he felt that there could always be the chance that abroad he could be seized by Russian agents in some way as an iron curtain defector. He wasn't even too sure about how safe Wales would be which was a slightly irrational fear, but he felt uneasy crossing the border into Wales that was technically another country. As a result of this he did not consider travelling back to Hungary until after the fall of the Berlin Wall in November 1989 and the subsequent fall of communism in Hungary. It was not until 1991 that Leo was ready to return to Hungary, driven by the desire to see his sister Magdi, her daughter Zuzsanna (Zuzsa) and his cousins Lali, Babus and their families. It had been some forty-five years since they had met and much had passed in the intervening years.

In 1990 Leo became a grandfather for the first time when Nick's wife Lorraine gave birth to a son named after him, Leo Nicholas Michael. Nick and Lorraine gave Leo and Anne another grandson in 1992, Joshua Seaton. In 1998 Bebba and her husband Charlie gave Leo and Anne their first granddaughter, Georgina. Joe and his wife Lisa gave them another two granddaughters, Jessica in 2003 and Isabel in 2006.

Anne accompanied Leo to Hungary in 1991 to meet the family.

After Leo had made this trip and realised that travelling abroad was now 'safe' he and Anne enjoyed many foreign holidays in France and eventually as far afield as Australia in 2007 to visit George who had been there on a yearlong working holiday.

In 1999 Leo took Nick to Hungary to meet family and proudly showed him around the sights of Budapest and

Hungary in general. Many of the locations mentioned earlier in this book were visited including the house where he lived as a child in Arcs, the Korvin cinema that he defended in 1956, his university, Gyor and Kunszentmarton, the location of the family crypt.

Leo's Hungarian family found it amusing that he had developed such English manners, especially his table manners which had become very stiff and formal. The Hungarian way at table is to just dig in and eat, drink, and enjoy without standing on ceremony. He had also become a great tea drinker which is not a Hungarian habit. They like their coffee which is peculated in cafetières, but most Hungarians do not have kettles, so Leo's tea water needed to be boiled up in pans on a stove, a constant source of fun for the family. Another taste Leo had developed in England was a love of cider. It's peculiar in Hungary that they can turn their hand to turning any fruit or vegetable into a fermented alcohol product (legally or otherwise), but the idea of turning apples into a drink that isn't a liquor is amusing and alien to them. They joked it was apple beer.

Leo returned to Hungary on a regular basis with various combinations of Nick, Joe, George, and Nick's son Leo (junior) to visit family, see the country and eat and drink to excess enjoying the famous, often too much, Hungarian hospitality.

Leo's last visit to Hungary was for his 80th birthday in 2013, this time with Nick and Joshua. During this trip to Budapest Leo was still reasonably able bodied although he did get tired walking around the sights but was still able to out drink both Nick and Joshua and was using a catchphrase he'd used on previous trips of 'drink up, drink up', whilst waving his empty glass.

Leo didn't really relish the thought of retirement and managed to keep his roofing business going until the age of 76. However, this only came about due to his health. He had suffered a stroke and it was no longer possible to drive and shin up ladders onto roofs.

Conclusion

- **Project Start: 19th May 2015**
- **Completion and submission to publisher: 10th January 2022**
- **Countless exploratory visits to the pub, a magnitude of cider washed down to loosen the lips and endless re-writes later:**

A simple fact is that, prior to 2015, I didn't know much about my father at all. I don't think any of the family did. I find myself very fortunate that I had this time with him to get his words and memories consigned to print and discover a past that was locked away.

To begin with, I asked Dad to put down on paper what had happened throughout his life, so we had a starting point for this project. He returned a week later and showed me the synopsis he'd laboriously typed up with a single finger on the computer. I no longer have this file to reference, unfortunately, but it roughly contained two tiny paragraphs, maybe no more than 50 words and consisted of some of the following dialogue to the best of my memory:

I was born in Acs on November 18th, 1933. I grew up during the invasion of Hungary and was part of the revolution before finally coming to England, meeting my wife, and starting a family.

The End.

9th July 2015 – the first of three exploratory 'interviews' took place at the local pub, Dad and I lubricated with cider for each. Whilst not being a person comfortable with talking about his past, writing down of the answers to my questions seemed to stir many memories for him and these three interviews were the start of the following four years of work with him.

Realistically, Dad never really knew where the book should end and unfortunately, he passed away before its completion and left Nick and I to finish off the unfinished elements. Throughout all of this, we were assisted by our cousin Hugh who was able to make sense of the intended story and subtly change it to a more readable format. Dad wrestled with the idea of continuing to write up until the present day, but it was agreed the book would never be completed; neither I nor Dad thought it would take more than about six months initially. As Bebba rightly commented to the idea, the years that Dad spent in England were not intended to be captured in this book and were simply the wonderful, everyday story of a loving husband, father, grandfather, and companion who would never complain even when confronted with difficult personal or financial worries or, later in life, with a multitude of medical challenges and discomfort.

How did the events in this book mold Leo into the man that settled in England, married his wife Anne, forged numerous, lifelong friendships, and nurtured a loving family? It's difficult to say and make connections, but what the book doesn't convey is some of these nuances, passions and things that aggrieved him sorely. Those that knew Leo well will hopefully find some of these observations ring true, and for those unfortunate not to have met him or were too young to remember, they will hopefully paint some colourful, but by no means exhaustive pictures of the revolutionary refugee this book portrays.

Pubs & Alcohol: A lover of good, old fashioned British pubs and a keen cider drinker who would show great disdain to the serving bar tender in an establishment that did not offer a brand to his liking. Dad liked nothing more than chomping down on a good traditional pie, but woe betide the chef that didn't make a 'proper pie' and simply put a puff pastry lid on a stew. A keen whisky and Palinka drinker, forever telling us to sip and savour each wincing shot, which always fell on deaf ears.

Food:

A lover of simple food, and lots of it. An incredibly fast eater, his false teeth sometimes making excruciating noises when slurping soup or eating spaghetti. No food preparation in the kitchen could ever be achieved without Dad appearing out of nowhere, enquiring what was coming up and when he was going to be able to get at it. Often prone to having sandwiches with leftover roast gravy spread thickly across white bread with no other filling and disappearing off early to bed clutching half a packet of digestives with crumbs already on the side of his face.

Joking aside, he could cook up a devilishly sumptuous Hungarian Goulash, spending hours bent over the stove perfecting his signature dish (His secret recipe is included within this book) which the family would suitably demolish at the dining table.

Less of a household favourite was his 'everything but the kitchen sink', homemade, 'Rubbish Soup' which included any leftovers from previous meals. Dad had known great hardship in his past and this showed with this watery, salty concoction; barely a scrap of food was ever binned in our home, including bones. Ingredients would include veg, old roast potatoes, ancient pasta, or rice and even the discarded pastry from mums' pies. It never made him ill, but nothing would turn my stomach more than waking on a Saturday morning after a heavy previous night on the town, to the noxious aroma emanating throughout the entire house of chicken bones and old carcasses being boiled up at 7am. Who knows, maybe it was secret, passive aggressive payback for me drunkenly crashing around at three in the morning.

Owner of many clothes, wearer of few:

A room packed full of clothes held no challenge to Dad. Generally remaining in the same clothes and the same set of favourite items until they had to be washed or simply fell to pieces. Each year my mother would dutifully wrap another jumper and/or smart shirt up in Christmas paper, to be placed under the tree. Every year his wardrobes would become a little bit fuller with unworn, brand-new clothes. Jeans would become shorts, slowly cut down every year until they resembled little more than speedos and only being thrown away when a family member complained or simply discarded of when he wasn't looking. Mainly they were repurposed again as cleaning rags etc. It must be mentioned however that Dad could look very debonair and dashing when he made the effort.

Hoarder and Salvager:

Everything had another purpose; nothing could be thrown away. Sandals would be trimmed off to fit smaller sized feet, gardening gloves had to be kept regardless of holes and defects. Upon clearing out Dad's garage/greenhouse after his passing, I found no less than 84 gloves distributed through many storage areas, the vast majority being left-handed and threadbare. We always thought of my Mum as being a bit of a hoarder, but it turns out that Dad was just as bad, he just had a large garden, garage and sheds to secretly disguise and camouflage his sins.

Devout Gardener:

When not working or on family outings, Dad's refuge was his garden. Slowly downsizing from a 1.5-acre plot of land in Arundel that would have kept a full-time landscaper very busy, to a more modest, but still hugely demanding mature garden at his last residence in East Preston. As time and his age progressed, the enormous workload took a great toll on his back with the colder months causing him to retreat inside. His poor circulation causing hands like ice in the warmest of gloves (which he probably kept when they wore out).

Hater of Technology, especially mobile phones.

Regardless of your age, skills and lack of previous experience, nobody in this world can truthfully claim that they couldn't use a DVD player after staring at one for 10+ years with the remote control sitting right next to them. Nobody? Well, with one exception. Dad abhorred mobile phones and whilst always 'claiming' he had one, it was either never turned on and/or never charged and nearly always left dutifully on the house window ledge whenever he left the house.

A Keen Glider

Having flown gliders in Hungary during his national service, Dad was also a gliding instructor for a brief time after arriving in England. After an absence of nearly 40 years behind the control stick, he once again took to the skies in his early 80's for what was to be his final flight. Prior to take-off he confidently told me that he "knew exactly what he was doing as a glider was a glider at the end of the day". Shortly after landing he reported that it had been thrilling, but he hadn't anticipated the aircraft would have changed quite so much.

A Proud Patriot

Very proud of his heritage, Dad loved to take us back to Hungary to show us all the sights and landmarks and meet our distant relatives. No matter his age, as soon as the plane touched down on the tarmac at Ferenc Liszt (Budapest airport), he would turn into an excited little boy, brimming with energy and enthusiasm and ready to put us to shame in the bars and drinking establishments around the city always urging us to "drink up, drink up".

Dad knew when his end was in sight, spending many days sitting in the conservatory, looking out wistfully at the garden he spent all his time caring and nurturing. Wishing, I'm sure, he could be out there weeding, trimming, and clearing leaves if only his health would let him. It appeared he'd made peace with this departure (although he had told me in a cheerful conversation 15 years prior to this he wouldn't be around the following year and be long gone) and often said calmly this was ok and he'd had a wonderful life.

With his book and life story 98% finished, he finally passed away on the 31st of July 2019 surrounded by his family. We were all fortunate to have the chance to say goodbye together and he was finally laid to rest, not in his family crypt in Hungary, but two worlds apart at Slindon Church, West Sussex, England in the country he had called home since arriving in the winter of 1956 and referred to as "his new heaven".

Dad was buried, dressed in his gardening clothes, and accompanied by a printed 1st draft copy of 'Have you Got TitPaste?' for some late-night reading which he was so fond of doing, his gravestone bears the epitaph, 'A wonderful life'.

Author of conclusion - 'George Solti, January 2022'

BV - #0015 - 040522 - C0 - 216/138/14 - PB - 9781912713509 - Matt Lamination